ALL NEW 100 LITERACY HOURS

 Follows the NLS medium-term planning

 Differentiated lesson plans

 Photocopiable extracts

YEAR 2

David Waugh

CREDITS

Author
David Waugh

Consultant
Wendy Jolliffe

Series Designer
Joy Monkhouse

Editor
Roanne Charles

Illustrations
Beverley Curl

Designer
Catherine Mason

Assistant Editor
Aileen Lalor

Text © David Waugh
© 2005 Scholastic Ltd

Designed using Adobe InDesign

Published by Scholastic Ltd
Villiers House
Clarendon Avenue
Leamington Spa
Warwickshire CV32 5PR

www.scholastic.co.uk

Printed by Bell and Bain Ltd.

3 4 5 6 7 8 9   6 7 8 9 0 1 2 3 4

British Library Cataloguing-in-Publication Data
A catalogue record for this book is available from the British Library.

ISBN 0-439-971-667
ISBN 978-0439-97166-9

ACKNOWLEDGEMENTS

The publishers gratefully acknowledge permission to reproduce the following copyright material: **Bounty (UK) Ltd** for the use of a table of the meaning of popular names and the most popular boys' and girls' names from their website www.bounty.com © Bounty (UK) Ltd. **Laura Cecil Literary Agency** as representatives of the James Reeve Estate for the use of 'The Wind' by James Reeves from *Complete Poems for Children* © 1959, James Reeves (1959, William Heinemann Ltd). **David Greygoose** for the use of the poem 'The Farmer's Cat' after a translation by Xia Lu from the traditional Chinese which appeared in *The Works* compiled by Paul Cookson © 2002, David Greygoose (2002, Macmillan Children's Books). **Her Majesty's Stationery Office** for the use of a table of popular names from 1904 to 2003 from the Office of National Statistics website www.statistics.gov.uk © Crown copyright reproduced with the permission of the Controller of HMSO. **Xia Lu** for the use of the translation of the poem 'The Farmer's Cat' retold by David Greygoose from *The Works* compiled by Paul Cookson, translation © 2002, Xia Lu (2002, Macmillan Children's Books). **Judith Nicholls** for the use of 'Timeless' by Judith Nicholls from *Dragonsfire* by Judith Nicholls © 1990, Judith Nicholls (1990, Faber and Faber). **Penguin UK Ltd** for the use of extracts and illustrations from *The Worst Witch* by Jill Murphy. Text and illustrations © 1974, Jill Murphy (1974, Alison and Busby). **Penguin UK Ltd** for the use of 'A day in the life of Danny the cat' by Benjamin Zephaniah from *Talking Turkeys* by Benjamin Zephaniah © 1994, Benjamin Zephaniah (1994, Viking). **Rosemary Waugh** for the retelling of 'Cinderella', 'The Thick Fat Pancake', 'King Midas' and 'King Log and King Stork' by Rosemary Waugh © 2005, Rosemary Waugh (2005, previously unpublished).

Contents

ALL NEW 100 LITERACY HOURS: YEAR 2

About the series
The books in the updated *All New 100 Literacy Hours* series offer a set of completely new term-by-term lesson plans, complete with objectives and organisation grids and accompanied, where relevant with photocopiable texts and activity sheets. The series offers a core of material for the teaching of the English curriculum within the structure of the Literacy Hour, but now perfectly matches the recent NLS *Medium-Term Plans*, *Developing early writing*, and *Speaking, Listening and Learning* guidelines. The series also builds on current teaching ideas including providing activities to match children's preferred learning styles.

Using this book
The units of work
This book provides 100 literacy hours for Year 2 based on the NLS *Medium-Term Plans*, which either form a core scheme of work or can be used to supplement your existing planning. This core should be extended in several ways. For example:
● The patterns of working in several of the units could be used as a template for work on other texts chosen by the teacher. For example, the Term 3 unit on the brothers Grimm could be adapted for work on Hans Christian Andersen or could be extended to explore other stories by the Grimms or other traditional tales.
● The poetry units in Term 1 could be extended to incorporate other verse forms on the theme of wind and weather.
  Additional time can be provided for extended writing. Several units include lessons which focus on extended writing, but these could be supplemented with further lessons in which text and word/sentence level work is minimal in order to release time for longer periods of independent working.
● Units could be extended to enable children to produce more polished final pieces of work such as displays, booklets and even websites. For example, the work on Victorians or wildflowers in Term 3 could be linked to work in history and science respectively, and could lead to extended cross-curricular work.
  In addition to the above, tried-and-tested resources from previous schemes of work, other publications, or the original *100 Literacy Hours* series, can be used to supplement the new materials.

The lesson plans
The lesson plans should be seen as a source of ideas, not as a straitjacket, and should therefore be used flexibly. Most lessons plans can easily be adapted for rotational use by alternating the independent and guided activities. The number of guided activities that are possible in one week will depend on the number of available adults. When planning rotation, it is important to ensure that all children experience

the key activities throughout the week. If following the linear model, guided activities will usually need to involve a guided version of the independent activity, otherwise children may miss out on key experiences.

Organisation of teaching units

Each term is divided into teaching units comprising between 5 and 10 hours. Each of the units cluster the NLS text-, sentence- and word-level objectives. The units are organised as follows:

Unit overview

Introduction
Overview of each unit including ideas for extending units.

Organisation grid
Outlines the key activities for each lesson.

Key assessment opportunities
A bulleted list of key assessment opportunities. These will help you to plan assessment opportunities throughout each unit.

Unit lesson plans

Each unit of lesson plans is written with the following headings:

Objectives
NLS objectives including Speaking and Listening emphases.

What you need
Provides a list of resources required for each lesson.

Shared work
Sets out the shared text-, sentence- and word-level work in each lesson. Some of these objectives are taught discretely, while others are integrated into the theme of the unit as the NLS recommends.

Guided and independent work
Every unit contains at least two suggestions for guided work to be used if the lessons plans are reorganised on a rotational basis. The lessons also include ideas for independent group, paired or individual activities. In some units, you may wish to re-organise these, along with the suggestions for guided work, on a rotational basis, for example, when a group set of books is being shared around the class.

Plenary
Sets out what to do in the whole-class plenary session.

Differentiation
Ideas for supporting more or less able children including ideas for peer and other adult support.

Links to the NLS Medium-term plans

The units provide clear links to the requirements of the NLS *Medium-Term Plans*. Genres are matched exactly with appropriate texts for the age group and the range of objectives covered, as shown on the grid for each term. Some of the word- and sentence-level objectives identified in the *Medium-Term Plans* have been relocated from the specified units to meet the needs of specific texts and the running order of the selected units.

Differentiation

In every lesson plan, suggestions for supporting the less able and stretching the more able are given. However, it is important to use these advisedly as a child may be 'less able' in some aspects of literacy, but 'more able' in others. These suggestions should be applied when appropriate to the individual child and not be automatically given to a predetermined group. Other important considerations are children's different learning styles, and the concept of 'multiple intelligences'. Children also need to experience working individually, in pairs, and in a range of larger groups, organised in different ways to meet different educational objectives. The number of groups will depend on class size, spread of ability and learning style. Try to ensure a balance of gender and personality type in each group, and don't hesitate to separate children who cannot work well together.

Assessment

Each unit includes a list of bullet points to help with ongoing assessment. These are not intended to replace National Curriculum assessment, but represent the 'bottom line' that all the children should have achieved by the end of the unit. If a number of children have failed to achieve satisfactory standards in any of the bulleted areas, then the unit may need to be revisited (with different resources).

Using the photocopiable resources

Where there is an instruction to copy material from copyright texts, you must ensure that this is done within the limits of the copying licence of your school. If pupils are using their own exercise books or paper for answers, then all photocopiable resources are reuseable.

Usually, the best way to share a resource with the class is to make a display version for an overhead projector or data projector. However, try to avoid this becoming routine. An effective alternative is to sit with the children in a circle and to work with a hard copy of the text and where possible, engage the children with actual books.

Interactive whiteboard use

Permission is granted for those pages marked as photocopiable to be used in that way. Where third party material is used, permission for interactive whiteboard use must be obtained from the copyright holder or their licensor. This information can be found in the acknowledgements at the front of the book.

Speaking and listening

When speaking and listening is one of the main focuses of the lessons, links are made to the Primary National Strategy's *Speaking, Listening and Learning* (DfES, 2003), and to the speaking and listening emphases within the *Medium-Term Planner*. These links are also highlighted in the objectives grid through the use of a logo ⌐⌐.

Children will use speaking and listening as a process skill in every lesson. If this is well organised, they will improve their speaking and listening skills *and* learn better. To encourage this, particular emphasis is given to children working with 'talk partners'. When a larger group is needed, 'talk partners' can join into fours. Groups of this size are ideal for discussion and collaborative work as they provide a range of opinion and yet are not too large to make full participation difficult. It is important to vary group organisation so that children experience working with different partners with different approaches or abilities.

Creativity

Recent reports have emphasised the importance of creativity and creativity is embedded within many of the lessons this book. Also encourage creativity by using some of the following ideas:

- Children as Real Writers - encourage children to see themselves as real writers writing for real purposes. This means giving them a strong sense of audience and purpose, using redrafting techniques and finding a way of 'publishing' completed work.
- Writing Journals - encourage the children to write something in their journal every day. This can be anything they like - diary entry, story, poem, exploration of a problem and so on. This is the one place where grammar, and punctuation do not matter. The aim is to develop writing fluency, that is, a free flow between thought and written page.
- First-Hand Experiences – many NLS writing tasks are responses to texts. Balance this by using stimulating 'real-life' starting points such as visits, visitors, artefacts, etc.
- Experimentation - encourage the children to play with ideas, and explore alternatives. Positively encourage them to suggest alternative tasks.
- Writing Materials – provide inspiring media such as paper in various colours and sizes; a variety of pens and pencils (for example felt-tipped pens, calligraphic pens); rulers; scissors; glue; DTP and presentation software; a clip art library; a colour printer.

Learning styles

Researchers have identified three different learning styles: auditory, kinaesthetic and visual. Most children will use a mixture of all three styles, but in some children, one style will predominate. Many lessons in this book offer specific opportunities for different learning styles, however, it is useful to keep in mind at all times the needs of each learning style:

Visual learners
- learn by seeing and looking
- benefit from illustrations, diagrams and presentations
- are helped by visual text analysis techniques such as annotation.

Auditory learners
- learn by hearing and listening
- acquire knowledge by reading aloud, reciting and repeating
- are helped by clear verbal explanations and discussion.

Kinaesthetic learners
- learn by touching and doing
- rely on what they can directly experience or perform
- are helped by physically manipulating things.

Media and ICT

There have been major advances in media and ICT. For this reason, we need to give more emphasis to media education and ICT in the primary classroom. This can be done by showing film versions of books and documentaries on non-fiction topics. Most children are now able to access the internet at home, and most schools have internet access. In school, the data projector and interactive whiteboard are replacing the blackboard and OHT. It may seem challenging to integrate ICT into your literacy teaching. Think of simple ways to use it every day, for example, allowing children to use the internet and CD-ROMs for research, and ensuring that, every time writing takes place, at least one group is using a word-processor.

Medium-term plan/ All New 100 Literacy Hours unit	Text level	Sentence level	Word level	Number of hours	Text(s)	Links to DEW, PiP Steps, S&L	Outcome
Narrative 1	T4 T5 T6 T11	S2 S3	W7 W10	5	The first day in Year 2' by David Waugh	DEW: unit A PIPs: step 7 S&L: 13–16	Relating story to own experiences. Role-play. Written retelling of story
Poetry	T7 T9 T12	S3 S4 S5	W1 W2 W3 W4 W11	10	'The Wind' by James Reeves; 'Windy Nights' by Robert Louis Stevenson; 'Who Has Seen the Wind?' by Christina Rossetti; 'Flying' by JM Westrup	PIPs: step 7 S&L: 13–15	Learning and reciting poems. Writing own verses on similar themes. Class display.
Non-fiction 1: Instructions	T11 T13 T14 T15 T16 T17 T18	S2 S5 S6	W6 W10	5	Sets of instructions in a variety of forms	S&L: 14, 15	Following instructions. Creating own instruction texts
Narrative 2	T2 T4 T5 T6 T7 T10 T11	S1 S3 S4 S5 S7	W1 W3 W7	10	'A walk in the dark woods' by David Waugh; 'Timeless' by Judith Nicholls	DEW: unit A PIPs: step 7 S&L: 13–16	Own stories inspired by texts read and own experiences
Non-fiction 2: Instructions	T11 T13 T14 T15 T16 T17	S4 S6	W10	5	Pictorial set of instructions	S&L: 14	Following and evaluating instructions. Own sets of instructions

Medium-term plan/ *All New 100 Literacy Hours* unit	Text level	Sentence level	Word level	Number of hours	Text(s)	Links to DEW, PiP Steps, S&L	Outcome
Narrative 1	T4 T5 T6 T7 T12	S2 S5 S6 S8 S9	W10	5	'Cinderella' by Rosemary Waugh	**DEW:** units B and E **S&L:** 13	Retelling of traditional tale. Character profiles.
Poetry	T2 T8 T9 T15	S1 S5 S7	W4 W10	5	'A Day in the Life of Danny the Cat' by Benjamin Zephaniah; 'The Farmer's Cat' by David Greygoose	**PiPs:** step 7	Own poems about cats. Class display.
Categorising alphabetically	T16 T17 T18 T20	S4 S5 S9	W3 W5	5	Charts of statistics of popular names; glossaries of names' meanings	**PiPs:** steps 5 and 7	Investigation into popular names and meanings of own names.
Narrative 2	T1 T2 T3 T4 T6 T7	S1 S5 S6 S9	W2 W3 W5 W8	10	'The Thick Fat Pancake', 'King Midas' and 'King Log and King Stork' by Rosemary Waugh	**S&L:** 16, 17, 18, 24	Retelling of story. Evaluation of stories.
Explanation	T1 T2 T19 T21	S6 S7 S9	W6 W9 W10	5	Short story about organising a birthday party; flow chart for planning a party	**PiPs:** step 7	Flow chart or diagram of plans for giving a birthday party or birthday present.

Medium-term plan/ *All New 100 Literacy Hours* unit	Text level	Sentence level	Word level	Number of hours	Text(s)	Links to DEW, PIP Steps, S&L	Outcome
Narrative 1	T1 T2 T4 T5 T9 T10	S1 S3 S5	W1 W2 W4 W7 W8 W9	10	'The Elves and the Shoemaker' and 'The Musicians of Bremen' by Jacob and Wilhelm Grimm	DEW: unit D PIPs: step 7 S&L: 13, 15, 24	Evaluation and retelling of stories. Own stories
Non-fiction 1	T1 T13 T14 T16 T17 T18 T20	S4 S5 S6	W9	5	Descriptions of common wild flowers	DEW: units G and I PIPs: steps 6 and 7	Class information booklet
Poetry	T1 T8 T9 T11	S1 S2	W1 W6 W9 W11	5	Traditional tongue twisters	DEW: unit 14 PIPs: step 5	Class anthology of tongue twisters
Narrative 2	T1 T2 T5 T7 T12	S1	W2 W9 W10	5	*The Worst Witch* by Jill Murphy	S&L: 13	Evaluation of book, relating it to other books
Non-fiction 2: Report	T1 T9 T13 T14 T16 T17 T19 T20	S4 S5 S6	W9 W10	10	Pictures and non-chronological reports about Victorian school and home life	DEW: unit H S&L: 21, 23	Notes Non-chronological report with subheadings

UNIT 1

Narrative 1

This unit on narrative is based upon a two-part story that relates to the children's own experiences of a first day in a new class. It should provide lots of opportunities for children to work in pairs and to recall and recount a story. The children will develop an understanding of the rules for adding -ing and will develop an understanding of words and phrases that link sentences and indicate time. This unit also covers *Developing early writing*, unit A and *Progression in phonics*, step 7.

Hour	Shared text-level work	Shared word-/ sentence-level work	Guided work	Independent work	Plenary
1 The first day in Year 2	Reading the first part of the story and relating it to own experiences.	Using awareness of grammar to decipher new words.	Talking and planning for writing about starting Year 2.	Writing sentences using new words learned.	Using word cards as prompts to retell story.
2 Constructing a plan for writing.	Environmental print trail.	Bingo game of high frequency words.	Planning for writing.	Planning for writing	Sharing plans and experiences. Matching *ing* word cards.
3 Exclamations	Reading the second part of the story. Identifying the function of exclamation marks. Hot-seating characters.	Revising -ing words. Collating a word bank of difficult words.	Writing focusing on adapting notes and using punctuation.	Beginning to write stories.	Noting punctuation in own writing. Reading with expression.
4 Linking sentences	Retelling part 2 of the story, using link words and phrases.		Continuing writing, introducing link words.	Continuing writing, introducing link words.	Sharing stories in pairs then as a class. Spotting link words used.
5 Finishing the story	Re-reading the whole story. Sharing experiences and ideas.	Using initial phonemes to find words in a word bank. Revising exclamation marks and commas.	Discussing and revising work.	Continuing extended writing.	Reading aloud. Reinforcing use of punctuation.

Key assessment opportunities
● Can the children relate the story to their own experiences?
● Do they use context to decipher new words?
● Do they understand how root words may change when -ing is added?
● Do they take punctuation into account when reading?
● Can they use words and phrases that link sentences?

The first day in Year 2

Objectives

NLS
T6: To discuss familiar story themes and link to own experiences.
W10: To learn new words from reading linked to particular topics.

S&L
14 Listening: To listen to others in class, ask relevant questions.

What you need

● Photocopiable page 17
● cloze sentences that could contain the words at the top of photocopiable page 19
● cards of the six words at the top of photocopiable page 19.

Differentiation

Less able
● Give children a series of sentences with spaces to be filled by using the new words.

More able
● Ask children to discuss and begin to plan stories about their first day in school.

Shared text-level work

● Begin by reading the first part of 'The first day in Year 2'.
● Discuss the sequence of events. What happened first? What happened when the children went into the cloakroom? Relate these to the children's own experiences by asking the children about their memories of their first day at school and then their first day in their present class. How did they feel? Were they nervous? What can they remember about the day?
● Read the text again. Ask the children why they think Mrs Smith has asked Kate to stand up. Has she done something wrong? Can they remember feeling nervous like Kate on their first day at school or in a new class? Can they tell you about a similar event?

Shared word-level work

● Discuss words in the passage that were new to the children. Write the words on the board and ask the children to make up sentences to include a few of words.
● Show the word cards and then write some more sentences, leaving spaces where missing words could be. Ask the children to look at the whole sentence before predicting what the missing word might be, for example:

> I was so ___ when I saw the monster that I couldn't stop shaking.
> Tom had to stand up because he ___ to Jo during ___.

Guided and independent work

● Work with a lower ability group to discuss their own first day at school as part of planning for writing. Prompt them to talk about what happened first, which other children they can remember and what they can recall about their teacher and the classroom. Discuss how they felt – whether they were worried, scared or excited. Ask them to talk in pairs and then as a group.
● Most will probably have been in the same class so tell them to remind each other and ask questions about events.
● Write some key words, which they mention and may need later, on a large sheet of paper.
● For independent work, leave the list of new words discussed in shared work on the board and ask the children to work in pairs to think of sentences that could use the new words they have learned. Encourage them to add the words to their spelling logs, discuss their meanings and practise spelling them.

Plenary

● Arrange the word cards in the order in which they appear in the story. Share some of the sentences that include the words and from this, retell the story.

Planning for writing

Objectives

NLS
T6: To discuss familiar story themes and link to own experiences.
W7: To use word endings, eg *ing* (present tense) to support their reading and spelling.
W10 To learn new words from reading linked to particular topics.

What you need
● As for Hour 1 plus *-ing* word cards from photocopiable page 19
● examples of words that can be modified by adding *-ing* from photocopiable page 19.

Shared text-level work

● Display photocopiable page 17 and recap the story.
● Explain that there is a second part to the story, but that first, the children are going to plan to write about their own experiences.
● Share some of the plans produced yesterday by more able children, and discuss the list of useful words produced with the guided group.
● Use the children's ideas to construct a plan for writing about a first day in a new class. Ask for suggestions for what should go at the beginning of the plan, for example, *waited in playground*, and show them how notes can be made concisely in single words or short phrases. Ask what would be the best way to order their story, and how they might end it.
● Recall some of the new words learned yesterday and encourage the children to incorporate these in the writing.

Shared word-level work

● Talk about some of the words that end in *-ing* in the shared text produced. Ask the children to tell you what the root words were before *-ing* was added, and list these on the board.
● Provide some examples of words that could be modified by adding *-ing* (changing active verbs to participles), for example *play, stay, look* and *read*.
● Now show words that require adjustment when *-ing* is added, such as *hide, write, hit* and *hop*. Talk about rules for dropping *e* and for doubling the consonant when a single vowel precedes the consonant, as *i* in *hit*, *e* in *let*, *a* in *bat*, *u* in *rub*, and *o* in *hop*.

Guided and independent work

● Ask children to plan for writing a story about a first day at school. This can be a true story about their own first day in a class, but they may embellish it by adding fictional elements if they wish. For example, they could change details about the setting or add some different characters. Encourage them to be as creative and imaginative as they like, while retaining the basic structure and subject matter of the story.
● Encourage children to use note form and to refer to the board for ideas if necessary.
● As independent work, children who began planning in the previous lesson could begin to write their stories.

Differentiation

Less able
● Ask children to work in pairs and to draw upon the list produced the previous day.

More able
● Give children a set of words that could be modified by adding *-ing* and ask them to change them.
● They could go on to write the new words in sentences to be included in their stories.

Plenary

● Discuss children's plans for writing and share ideas and experiences.
● Give out the two sets of word cards from photocopiable page 19. Ask children to take turns to hold up their cards, then invite the child with the matching word to hold theirs up too, for example *like* and *liking*.
● Discuss what happened to the original word when *-ing* was added. Was the *e* dropped? Was the consonant doubled? Did the word remain the same?

Exclamations

Shared text- and sentence-level work
● Show the children the first part of 'The first day in Year 2' and ask them to remind each other of the story so far.
● Ask one child to play the role of Kate. Then say the lines that Mrs Smith said at the end of part 1. Ask 'Kate' how she felt and what she thought might happen next. Encourage her to answer in role.
● Explain that photocopiable page 18 is the second part to the story and that the children will find out what happened to Kate. Tell them that you will be inviting Kate to answer questions in role and that you also need someone to play the part of Jack.
● Read the story with the children.
● Emphasise the role of commas, full stops and exclamation marks when reading aloud. Talk about why we use exclamation marks. (To indicate commands, or emotions such as joy, anger, surprise or humour.) Say a few sentences expressively and ask the children to discuss in pairs whether they should be written with or without exclamation marks. For example, *Quick, shut the door! I like fish fingers. Stop it at once! Paris is in France.*
● Ask the children to take turns to re-read the sentences in the story that include exclamation marks.
● Now let the class ask Kate and Jack questions and discuss the answers. Hotseat other children as the same or other characters.

Shared word-level work
● Talk about some of the words from the text that end in -*ing* and see if the children can tell you what the root words were.
● Make a word bank of unfamiliar words from the story.

Guided and independent work
● Work with a middle-ability group. Refer to the plans they made in the previous lesson, and discuss how they can best turn their notes into complete sentences.
● Demonstrate that punctuation helps the reader to understand the text, and that incorrect punctuation can lead to confusion. Write some incorrectly punctuated sentences on the board in order to show this.
● In independent work, ask children to use the plans they made in the previous lesson to begin writing their stories.
● Encourage children to think carefully about punctuation and to consider using exclamation marks where appropriate. Explain that they will be able to continue their stories in the next lesson.

Plenary
● Ask children to find examples of different punctuation marks in their writing. Invite children to read sentences that include the punctuation marks to show that they understand their functions.
● Emphasise the importance of reading the sentences with appropriate expression for punctuation. Encourage the children to read aloud in order to consolidate their knowledge of punctuation.

Objectives

NLS

T11: To use language of time to structure a sequence of events.

S2: To find examples in fiction of words and phrases that link sentences.

S&L

15 Group discussion and interaction: To listen to each other's views and preferences.

What you need

● Photocopiable pages 17 and 18.

Linking sentences

Shared text- and sentence-level work

● Question the children about the sequence of events in the story 'The first day in Year 2'. Ask them to remember the important events. Write these on the board, deliberately making occasional mistakes in the sequence and allowing the children to correct them.

● Look at the story, paying particular attention to words and phrases that link sentences, such as *when, next* and *before long.* Talk about the way in which such words and phrases help us to link a sequence of events. Why is it important to link different events in this way?

● Ask the children to talk about the stories they began to write in the previous lesson, and ask them to share any parts that they were particularly pleased with and might be able to contribute to a class story.

● With the children's help, begin to write the next part of the story. As you write, talk about punctuation and spellings and encourage children to suggest words which could link the sentences and show the passage of time. Note these on the board, asking the children what they particularly like about the words.

● Re-read their story and encourage the children to discuss ways in which it might be developed and improved. Make occasional deliberate mistakes and encourage children to spot these and to correct them.

Guided and independent work

● Ask the children to continue their stories about a first day at school. Tell them to spend time discussing their stories with partners, share ideas and compare the ways in which they have recorded their ideas.

● Encourage them to make use of words and phrases that link sentences and help us to structure a story. Ask them to help each other to include these in their stories where appropriate.

● Guide children's writing of their version of the final part of the story. Focus in particular on words and phrases that link sentences and indicate a change in time. Encourage the children to think about past, present and future tense and ask them to share examples of sentences in different tenses with the group.

Differentiation

Less able

● Provide children with some examples of linking words and phrases (*after, before, then, next* and so on) but ask them if they can find others.

More able

● Ask children to list words and phrases and then to use them in their stories to show a sequence of events.

Plenary

● Ask children to read their stories to each other and to discuss the events so far and what might happen next. Encourage them to offer each other ideas.

● Choose some children to read their stories to the class.

● Ask other children to spot linking words and phrases that the writer-reader found and try to use these in new sentences.

● Write examples of linking words on card and display them so that children can look for examples when reading independently.

● Ask children about their own feelings on starting in a new class. Were they frightened? Excited? Write these feelings on the board and look for suggestions of how they might convey them in their stories.

Finishing the story

Objectives

NLS
T4: To understand time and sequential relationships in stories, ie what happened when.
S3: To recognise and take account of commas and exclamation marks in reading aloud with appropriate expression.

S&L
13 Speaking: To speak with clarity and use intonation when reading and reciting texts.

What you need
● Photocopiable pages 17 and 18
● bank of words and phrases that link sentences and indicate a change of time (*after, before, then, next* and so on).

Differentiation

Less able
● Organise children to work with more able writing partners to produce joint pieces of writing based upon their shared ideas.

More able
● Ask children to prepare to read their work aloud during the plenary.

Shared text-level work
● In this final session, the children will be continuing their extended writing. They will need to revisit the story and revise some of the vocabulary encountered during the week.
● Read the whole story again with the children.
● Talk about the guided writing they have already done, and explain that they will be continuing to write about a first day in a new class during the lesson.
● Discuss the children's own experiences and share some of the ideas they have used in their writing.
● Ask children to think about the stories they have been writing and to consider what they still need to write about to complete them. Encourage them to discuss this in pairs and then ask volunteers to tell the class what they intend to write next.
● With the children's help, write some sentences on the board that will help children to articulate their ideas when completing their stories. Include words and phrases from the word bank.

Shared sentence-level work
● Talk about the words in the word bank and show the children how to use the initial sounds of the words to locate the ones they need.
● Remind the children about the use of exclamation marks and commas and encourage them to use these correctly in their writing. Explain that exclamation marks should be used sparingly so that their impact is greater. Show some samples of correct usage, for example, from comics and books. Ask children to look at these and to try saying the lines with appropriate intonation and expression.

Guided and independent work
● Work with a group of more able children to encourage discussion about their writing and to help them to edit and revise their work.
● Let children continue and complete their writing about the first day in a new class.
● Encourage them to re-read their work and to practise reading it aloud with appropriate intonation and expression.
● Allow children to use a desktop publishing package to write out their stories. Add the children's scanned artwork or ClipArt pictures and put the stories together as a class book.

Plenary
● Ask children to choose extracts from their stories to read to partners and to the class. Encourage them to read clearly and with appropriate expression and intonation.
● Write some examples of unpunctuated sentences on the board and ask the children to suggest where punctuation marks should be placed. In particular, provide sentences which might need an exclamation mark to add impact. Remind children that some punctuation rules are strict and some, such as placement of commas, are at the writer's discretion.

The first day in Year 2 – part 1

As we lined up on the playground, I began to feel even more nervous than before. All through the holiday I had been worrying about going into Mrs Smith's class. I had really liked being in Year One in Miss Patel's class. She was kind and smiled a lot, and she never shouted. Mrs Smith was the Deputy Headteacher and I had seen her telling people off for talking in assembly.

Mrs Smith stood at the front of our line and said, "Right Class 2S, I want you to set a good example to everyone else on the infant playground. You're the big ones now, and you have to show the younger children how to behave!"

We all walked smartly and very quietly to the cloakroom except Jack Kelly, who pushed Chloe White and made her cry. Mrs Smith saw what had happened and told Jack to wait behind. She knelt down next to Chloe and wiped her eyes with a tissue and whispered something to her. Chloe was smiling when she got to the cloakroom. I don't know what she said to Jack, but he was very quiet when he came into the cloakroom and he didn't misbehave again that day or the next day.

In the classroom Mrs Smith had put a small pile of exercise books in each person's place, and in each place there was also a piece of folded card with a child's name on it so that we could find our places. No one made a fuss, because Mrs Smith had told us that we were the oldest children in our part of the school and we had to show how grown up we were.

Everyone was trying really hard to be sensible and grown up. We began to write our names very neatly on each book as Mrs Smith had told us to.

Suddenly, we all stopped with our pencils in mid-air. "Kate Downing!" said Mrs Smith in a loud voice. "Stand up please!"

We all turned to look at Kate as she nervously stood up behind her desk.

The first day in Year 2 – part 2

"Hold up one of your books so that everyone can see it, Kate!" said Mrs Smith. "Now look everyone, that is exactly what I want you to do. Kate has written her name beautifully on her books and she has taken care to write very neatly. I want you to go over to the big yellow chart next to the whiteboard, Kate, and you can be the first person to earn a point for your table."

We all watched as Mrs Smith showed Kate how to put a blue sticker in the space next to the names of the people on her table. She showed us that there were spaces for children on all the tables to put stickers when they got points for doing good work or behaving well.

Before long, four more people had been given points for their tables and everyone worked really carefully, hoping that Mrs Smith would award more. Jack Kelly got a point for being the most sensible person in the class when we all went to sit on the carpet, and then Chloe got a point for being brave when Jack pushed her when we lined up. Jack apologised to Chloe and Mrs Smith gave him another point for being grown up enough to say he was sorry.

We all read the beginning of a story about a boy who got lost in a shop, and then we had to go back to our places and write sentences about the main characters. When we all came back to the carpet, Mrs Smith asked me to read some of my sentences to the class, and she even wrote one of them on the board and told everyone it was very good. When the bell went for assembly, I couldn't believe how quickly time had passed. Being in Mrs Smith's class seemed as if it might not be so bad after all!

Word cards

nervous	whispered	tissue	
assembly	sensible	nervously	
hide	run	work	fly
think	hop	tip	whisper
make	try	leave	eat
hear	love	skip	go
be	have	taste	hope
hiding	having	thinking	tasting
running	hoping	hopping	eating
working	making	tipping	hearing
flying	leaving	whispering	trying
being	loving	go	skip

Poetry

In this unit on poetry, children will look at a range of poems on a common theme: the wind. The poems have varying styles and rhyming sequences and are simple enough for children to be able to discern the pattern in each and replicate it in writing. The focus on rhymes provides a good opportunity to look at different spellings of phonemes and to revise common spelling patterns for long-vowel digraphs. This unit also covers *Progression in phonics*, step 7.

Hour	Shared text-level work	Shared word-/sentence-level work	Guided work	Independent work	Plenary
1 The Wind	Reading and reciting 'The Wind'.	Looking at new words. Focusing on words with long-vowel digraphs, noting spellings and sounds.	Re-reading the poem and writing own rhyming couplets about the wind.	Finding long-vowel digraphs in other texts. Sorting word cards by the sound of the long-vowel digraph.	Matching word cards to words on the board. Identifying sounds with various spellings.
2 Writing another verse	Re-reading 'The Wind'. Sharing ideas for another couplet.	Finding rhymes for long-vowel digraphs related to the wind.	Writing couplets about the wind.	Matching rhyming words. Writing couplets about the wind.	Sharing couplets. Focusing on long-vowel digraphs and rhymes.
3 Windy Nights	Reading 'Windy Nights'.	Looking at words that have the same sounds represented by different letters.	Writing another verse for 'Windy Nights'.	Looking in reading books for words with the same sounds but different spellings.	Reading and discussing new verses, focusing on rhyme.
4 Capital letters	Looking at the structure of the poem. Writing additional lines.	Identifying uses of capital letters in prose and poetry.	Writing another verse for 'Windy Nights'	Finding capital letters in texts and explain why they are used.	Discussing different uses of capital letters.
5 Writing wind poems	Revisiting both poems. Shared writing of new poems.	Revisiting both poems. Shared writing of new poems.	Writing wind poems.	Writing wind poems.	Sharing poems, focusing on spelling and discussing how punctuation affects reading.

UNIT 2

Hour	Shared text level work	Shared word/ sentence level work	Guided work	Independent work	Plenary
6 Who Has Seen the Wind?	Reading 'Who Has Seen the Wind?'. Help children to learn the poem by heart and to recite it. Discussing imagery.	Looking at *ea* and *ou* words.	Reading with expression and intonation.	Writing a new verse, focusing on rhymes. Learning for recitation.	Reciting the poem and new verses.
7 A good moon: the *oo* digraph	Re-reading 'Who Has Seen the Wind?' and writing an extra verse.	Collecting words that rhyme with *you*. Looking at different spellings of the *oo* sound, and different sounds made by *oo* spelling.	Writing of additional verses.	Playing a card game to sort *oo* words.	Sharing new verses. Playing another game on *oo* words.
8 Flying	Reading 'Flying'. Discussing similes and imagery.	Looking at rhymes in the poem. Classifying words with the same sounds but different spellings.	Re-reading the poem with expression.	Making collections of rhyming words. Writing the beginning of a poem set on a windy night.	Sharing new lines. Revising rhymes and thinking of more for using in Hour 9.
9 The moon on a windy night	Writing a poem similar to 'Flying', then reading and editing it.	Discussing rhyming words collected so far.	Continuing writing lines.	Continuing writing. Collecting rhyming words.	Reading aloud. Practising spelling of rhyming words.
10 Evaluating the poems	Re-reading and comparing the four poems.	Looking at the uses of rhymes and capital letters in the poems.	Writing or continuing poems about the wind.	Using a structure to write new poems about the wind.	Sharing the children's poems. Arranging a topic display.

Key assessment opportunities
● Can the children read and recite poems, paying attention to punctuation and rhyme?
● Have they used simple poetry structures to write their own poems?
● Do they use phonological and graphical knowledge to spell words?
● Do they understand that words with the same sounds may be spelled differently?
● Is their knowledge of long-vowel digraphs secure?

The Wind

Objectives

NLS
T7: To learn, re-read and recite favourite poems, taking account of punctuation; to comment on aspects such as word combinations, sound patterns (such as rhymes, rhythms).
W1: To secure identification, spelling and reading of long-vowel digraphs in simple words.

S&L
13 Speaking: To speak with clarity and use intonation when reading and reciting texts.

What you need

● Photocopiable page 32
● cards of long-vowel digraphs from enlarged photocopiable page 34.

Shared text-level work

● Read 'The Wind' to the children. Do not tell them the title, and see if they can guess the subject of the poem. If necessary, help them with the unusual sentence construction in line 5.
● Talk about how the poem is set out: in four sets of rhyming couplets. Ask the children to spot the rhyming pairs.
● Distribute photocopiable page 32. Discuss how James Reeves describes the power of the wind in terms of its effects on different things, such as trees, towers and the sea. Notice the powerful verbs and the quick rhythm, making use of short words.
● Help the children to learn the poem by saying one couplet at a time with them and asking them to repeat it. Try covering the poem and then reading it to the children, but leave out a little more each time and ask them to fill in the gaps.
● Recite the poem with the children when they know most of it.

Shared word-level work

● Discuss the meanings of unfamiliar words, such as *a pink, rave, riot, scent, spent*.
● Pick out words with long-vowel digraphs, such as *without, oak, leaves, house*. Ask the children if they can identify others in the poem.
● Ask the children to suggest other words they know with long vowel sounds. List them on the board and discuss their spellings. Sort the words into columns according to their long vowel sounds.

Guided and independent work

● Ask the children to read the poem and identify the words with long vowel sounds.
● Ask if they know others, not in the poem, that rhyme with those that are. Discuss different ways in which some long vowel digraphs can be written, for example *ou* and *ow; oi* and *oy; ea* and *ee*.
● Support the children as they write their own rhyming couplets about the wind. It may be necessary to give them a start by writing the first few words of the first line and asking them to complete it before reading their work aloud. Ask the group to help each other to think of rhymes for the second lines.
● Ask the children to notice words with long-vowel digraphs in reading books and to begin making a collection of rhyming words.
● Ask the children to sort the word cards into different sounds.

Differentiation

Less able
● Allow children to concentrate on reading and sorting the word cards.

More able
● Ask children to find and list other words with similar sounds to those from photocopiable page 34.

Plenary

● Give out the word cards with long-vowel digraphs so that each child has one word. Write the words on the board one at a time and ask the children to hold up their card if it matches yours or if it has the same long vowel sound.
● Look for signs that the children can identify similar sounds with different spellings.

Objectives

NLS
T12: To use simple poetry structures and to substitute own ideas, write new lines.
W3: To learn the common spelling patterns for the vowel phonemes.

What you need

● Photocopiable page 32
● word cards of long-vowel digraphs from enlarged photocopiable page 34.

Writing another verse

Shared text-level work

● Re-read 'The Wind' and revisit its structure.
● Explain that you would like the children to help you to write an additional couplet in the same style as James Reeves.
● Ask for suggestions for an opening line (clause). Remind the children that the poem is written in the first person as if the wind is writing about itself. Suggest that the opening line should, like Reeves' poem, tell of something the wind claims it can do. Ask the children to discuss their ideas in pairs before offering suggestions.
● Ask the children to think of rhymes for the word at the end of the line. Write their suggestions on the board. If the word has few possible rhymes within the 'wind' subject area, suggest they modify the line.
● Now ask children to suggest a second line. Ask them to re-read the first line before doing so and to discuss their ideas for a rhyming line with their partners.
● If time permits, or if you feel the children need it, repeat for another couplet.

Shared word-level work

● Together, think of rhymes for *oo*, *ar*, *oy*, *ee* and *ow* words that may be related to the wind, for example *cool*, *far*, *howl*, *feel* and *loud*. Explain that these will be useful when they write their own poems, as a bank of rhyming words on which to draw. Mention that if the digraph is not at the end of the word, the consonant after the digraph also makes the rhyme (*feel* and *feet* don't rhyme). Emphasise that words with similar sounds can have different spellings.
● Repeat the plenary activity from hour 1.

Guided and independent work

● Work with a group of children to help them write rhyming couplets about the wind. Begin by asking them to write as many words as they can think of that might be used in a poem about the wind, then ask them to share these with others to find rhymes.
● Ask the children to work in pairs to match rhyming words using the cards from photocopiable page 34.
● They can go on to brainstorm other words that rhyme with the words on the cards or write rhyming couplets for their wind poems. Remind them to include words containing long-vowel digraphs from the word bank on the board.

Plenary

● Share the children's couplets. Discuss the content, long-vowel digraphs and rhymes. Write some examples on the board and read them aloud with the children.
● Choose a few of the rhyming words and ask the children if they can suggest any other rhymes. Ask them to brainstorm as many words to fill the space as they can within a set period of time.

Differentiation

Less able
● Encourage children to work together to share and discuss ideas and ensure that they work with others who can provide support.

More able
● Provide a rhyming dictionary for children to extend the range of vocabulary they use.

UNIT 2 HOUR 3 📖 Poetry

Windy Nights

Objectives

NLS
T12: To use simple poetry structures and to substitute own ideas, write new lines.
W4: To investigate and classify words with the same sounds but different spellings.

What you need
● Photocopiable page 32
● the children's reading books.

Shared text-level work
● Tell the children that they are going to look at another poem about the wind. Show them 'Windy Nights'. Explain that it was written more than a hundred years ago and ask them to look out for any signs of this in the poem. They might spot the galloping man and the fires as references to a bygone age.
● Read the poem together and discuss it with them. Do they think that a man really gallops about whenever it is windy, or could this be a way of describing the noise made by the wind? Encourage the children to explain their ideas.

Shared word-level work
● Focus on words from the poem that have the same sounds represented by different letters, for example *high* and *by*, *sea* and *he*.
● Ask children to help you to write others. If they are short of ideas suggest *low* (*go, know, toe*), *loud* (*crowd, bowed*), *goes* (*nose, rows*).
● Talk about the different spellings which can often be used to represent the same sounds and write words in different lists according to their spellings. For example, words with *ow, o,* or *oe.*

Guided and independent work
● Work to write an additional verse for 'Windy Nights'. Discuss the rhyming pattern (ABABCC).
● Talk about the repetition of *whenever.* Why has the poet repeated this word?
● Discuss some of the interesting phrasing, such as *the wind is high* and *ships are tossed at sea.*
● As a starting point for independent work, draw upon rhyming words discussed in shared work, and those produced the previous day, and encourage children to think carefully about rhymes before they begin writing.
● Ask the children to look in their reading books for words with the same vowel sounds but different spellings. They should write down as many pairs as possible on individual pieces of paper, and work in pairs to sort them according to their sounds. For example, they may find *be/see, do/shoe, go/know, goes/knows, heard/bird.*
● Some may discover more than two words, in which case, ask them to record and sort these too.

Differentiation

Less able
● Ensure that children work together with more able readers and use simple texts to look for words.

More able
● Challenge children to find as many different spellings for the same sound as they can. For example, the *ee* sound in *bee* could be made with *ea* as in *read, ae* as in *encyclopaedia, ey* as in *key.*

Plenary
● Read some of the new verses the children have written, and discuss them alongside Stevenson's poem. Talk about the rhymes they have produced and pick out any words that have the same sounds written differently.
● Discuss the use of rhyming words in the poem and talk about the effect they have on the way in which we read it and remember it.
● Talk about the difference between prose and poetry – the rhyme and rhythm.

Capital letters

Objectives

NLS
T7: To learn, re-read and recite favourite poems, taking account of punctuation.
T12: To use simple poetry structures and to substitute own ideas, write new lines.
S5: To revise knowledge about other uses of capitalisation, eg for names, headings, titles, emphasis, and begin to use in own writing.

What you need

● Photocopiable page 32.

Shared text-level work

● Look again at the structure of 'Windy Nights'. Draw upon the children's previous discussions and let them talk to each other about this.
● Using the children's work, write some additional lines for the poem on the board, making some deliberate errors, in particular, miss out capital letters. Ask the children to point out the errors and how to correct them.

Shared word- and sentence-level work

● Discuss general uses of capital letters in titles of stories, poems, films and so on and for the names of people and places.
● Look at the use of a capital letter at the beginning of each line in this poem and 'The Wind'. Discuss how capital letters often begin the lines in poems but not in stories. Emphasise that every sentence in prose should begin with a capital letter, but that capital letters should only appear in the middle of sentences when used for names or for speech.
● Look at the following lines from the poem:

> All night long in the dark and wet,
> A man goes riding by.

Ask the children how you would write this if it was not part of a poem. Talk about it being one sentence which would be written as *All night long in the dark and wet a man goes riding by.*

Guided and independent work

● Work with a different group to write additional verses for the poem. Remind them that each line should begin with a capital letter.
● Draw upon the bank of rhyming words developed over the previous three lessons, but encourage children to think of other words which they could include.
● Ask the children to look in books and around the classroom at examples of capital letters. They should find examples of names, titles, beginnings of sentences. Ask them also to look for words in which all the letters are capital letters, such as labels and notices.
● Show the children how to use a chart with columns headed, for example, *names, sentences, titles, poems* to record examples. They should write each word they find in the appropriate column and note where they found it, for example *Asif (on his drawer)* under *names*, *Once (at the start of a book)* under *sentences*, *POETRY (on the wall display)* under *titles*.

Differentiation

Less able
● Ask children to begin by looking in simple reading books for words with capital letters.

More able
● Encourage children to look for further examples of capital letters in a range of texts, including directories and reference books.

Plenary

● Share some examples of the children's verses. Draw attention to interesting rhymes and the use of capital letters.
● Discuss some of the different uses of capital letters the children have found. Can they think of any more examples, such as adding emphasis in posters?

UNIT 2 HOUR 5 ▌ Poetry

Writing wind poems

Objectives

NLS

T12: To use simple poetry structures and to substitute own ideas, write new lines.

S3: To recognise and take account of commas and exclamation marks in reading aloud with appropriate expression.

S4: To re-read own writing for sense and punctuation.

S&L

14 Listening: To listen to others in class, ask relevant questions and follow instructions.

What you need

● Photocopiable page 32.
● mini whiteboards or paper on clipboards for pairs of children.

Differentiation

Less able

● Ask children to write very simple poems with only two or three words per line. For example, *Windy nights, Terrible sights, Falling trees, Choppy seas.*

More able

● Encourage children to write at greater length and to prepare to perform their poems, perhaps adding sound effects.

Shared text- and word-level work

● Show the children the two poems and re-read them.
● Ask the children which they prefer and why.
● Talk about the rhyme schemes in each poem and discuss the similarities and differences in structure, rhythm, imagery, vocabulary and so on.
● Tell the children that you are going to write new poems about the wind. Before beginning, remind them about the word bank of rhyming words begun in previous hours, as this will give them some ideas for the final words in each line.
● Explain that you want the children to discuss ideas for the poem and to think about how to set it out. Invite their suggestions and decide together which format to use. For example, four lines per verse, with lines 1 and 2 rhyming and 3 and 4 rhyming, or 1 rhyming with 3 and 2 with 4.
● Ask the children to make notes on their whiteboards towards writing the first line of the poem. Ask several pairs to say their lines and then ask the class to choose one as a starting point, reminding them that a rhyme will need to be found for the last word. Write the line on the board and then ask children to discuss in pairs what the next line might be and so on.
● Pause regularly to edit the lines.

Guided and independent work

● Ask the children to work in pairs to write their wind poems. The poems don't need to be very long and, for some children, they may be only two lines. Encourage the sharing of ideas, and ask children to show each other their work and discuss it at regular intervals as they write and edit.
● Work with the children to support their writing of wind poems. Discuss vocabulary, rhymes and phrasing and encourage them to draft, edit and revise their work following discussions with partners and with the group. Talk too about punctuation and the use of question marks and exclamation marks to indicate to the reader how the poem should be read.

Plenary

● Ask some children to read their poems aloud to the rest of the class. Discuss the rhymes they have used and write some on the board so that you can talk about spellings. Focus in particular on words that have the same sounds but different spellings.
● Discuss the punctuation in the poems and ask children to think about how this affects the way in which they should be read. Ask children to read each other's poems and ask the authors if the readers read them as they intended them to sound. Discuss the importance of presenting poetry so that others are interested in it and want to listen to it.
● Show some of the verses and look for correct use of capital letters.

Who Has Seen the Wind?

Objectives

NLS
T7: To learn, re-read and recite favourite poems.
W2: To revise and extend the reading and spelling of words containing different spellings of the long-vowel phonemes.
W11: To practise handwriting patterns from Year 1.

S&L
13 Speaking: To speak with clarity and use intonation when reading and reciting texts.

What you need
● Photocopiable page 33
● *ou* and *ea* word cards from enlarged photocopiable page 34
● tape recorders.

Differentiation

Less able
● See Guided and independent work

More able
● Encourage children to record their poems and discuss ways to improve the performances before re-recording them.

Shared text-level work
● Read 'Who Has Seen the Wind?' with the children.
● Help them to learn the poem by heart. Do this by learning a few lines at a time, then asking the children to work in pairs to take turns to see how much of each verse they can remember.
● Now focus on two lines: *But when the leaves hang trembling* and *But when the trees bow down their heads.* Talk about *trembling* and ask what it means. Demonstrate how one might tremble with fear and ask what the children think is happening to make the leaves seem to tremble. Discuss the idea of trees bowing their heads and ask if children can suggest what the author was trying to tell us by ascribing a human-type action to the trees.

Shared word-level work
● Look at *ea* and *ou* words in the first verse: *leaves, you* and *through.* Ask for other words which include these phonemes. Compare words that have *ea* or *ou* spellings but are pronounced differently, for example *heads* in the second verse.
● Hand out the word cards. They mainly focus on *ou* as in *you* or *noun*, and *ea* as in *head* or *real*. However, children will be aware of words such as *four* and *area* in which the digraph is different, so some words are included to allow for discussion about this. *Lead* and *lead* (a dog's lead and a lead weight) are included as examples of homographs.
● Write *ea* and *ou* words on the board, say them aloud, and ask the children to hold up their word cards if the *ea* or *ou* sound matches the word on the board. Include children's names where possible. If there are children in the class whose names include *ou* or *ea* but don't fit the pattern, such as Sean and Leanne, you should still discuss the names and their pronunciations.

Guided and independent work
● Work with a lower ability group to help them to learn the poem and read it with expression and intonation. Model expressive reading and talk about the importance of engaging an audience's interest.
● Ask children to work in pairs to write a new verse for 'Who Has Seen the Wind?'.
● Discuss rhymes with the children, and stop them occasionally to talk about spellings, focusing in particular on words which include *ea* and *ou.*
● Ask the pairs to write the poem out neatly, including their new verse, and to learn the poem to prepare for reciting to the class.

Plenary
● Ask children to read their verses aloud. Write examples on the board, modelling basic handwriting joins.
● Look for examples of rhyming words and words which include *ou* or *ea* and discuss their spellings with the class. Talk about words that have the same spelling pattern and sound different.

A good moon: the oo digraph

Objectives

NLS
T12: To use simple poetry structures and to substitute own ideas, write new lines.
W3: To learn the common spelling patterns for the vowel phoneme: *oo*; to identify the phoneme in speech and writing.

S&L
14 Listening: To listen to others in class, ask relevant questions and follow instructions.

What you need

● Photocopiable page 33
● cards of *oo* words from enlarged photocopiable page 34
● dictionaries.

Differentiation

Less able
● Children should play the games in mixed ability groups, but some could play with more able partners.

More able
● Encourage children to look for other words that include *oo* and to find out what they mean. They could do this by making up words and then checking in a dictionary to see if they exist.

Shared text-level work

● Re-read 'Who Has Seen the Wind?'.
● With the children's help, write an additional verse with the same style and structure. Begin with the first two lines of Rossetti's poem, then ask for suggestions for the next two. The final word should rhyme with *you*, so take suggestions for rhyming words before writing the lines.
● Ask pairs of children to discuss the ways in which we can see the effects of the wind, and note some of these on the board to help with the third line.
● Discuss the repetition at the beginning of the lines and the subtle change in the second verse (*Neither you nor I*), which enables the poet to make a different rhyme.

Shared word-level work

● Look at the vowel digraph *oo*. Ask the children if they can spot two words in the poem that have a similar sound to *oo* in *moon*. (*You* and *through*.) Explain that *oo* can also be pronounced as in *good*. Write *good* and *moon* on the board and ask the children to say each of them.
● Then ask the children to think of other *oo* words, for example, *book, cook, soon, food, look, boot*, and list them under *good* or *moon*.

Guided and independent work

● Work with a group to support their writing of an additional verse for the poem, in which the final word rhymes with *I*, as in Rossetti's second verse. Emphasise the importance of finding rhymes and ask everyone in the group for suggestions.
● As independent work, ask the children to sort the word cards into those with the *oo* sound as in *good*, and those with the *oo* sound as in *moon* by making two lists.
● They could go on to spread the word cards face down on the table and play a matching game with a partner or small group. Each player takes two cards. If the words have the same *oo* sound the player takes the 'trick'. If not, the words are turned over again and another player has a turn. When all the words have been taken, the player with the most pairs is the winner.

Plenary

● Ask children to read their verses to the class. Talk about the rhymes they have used.
● Give each child an *oo* word card. Ask children to take turns to stand up and show their cards and ask all of those who have the same *oo* sound to hold up their card.
● Take all the cards in and divide them into two equal piles. Ask two children to take the top card from each pile and hold them up. If the words have a matching *oo* sound the class can say *Snap*. If not, ask one child to take another word and see if that matches.

Flying

Objectives

NLS
T9: Through shared and guided writing to apply phonological, graphic knowledge and sight vocabulary to spell words accurately.
W4: To investigate and classify words with the same sounds but different spellings.

S&L
13 Speaking: To speak with clarity and use intonation when reading and reciting texts.

What you need
● Photocopiable page 33.

Shared text-level work
● Read 'Flying' to the children and then with them.
● Talk about the poem and ask the children about the poet's idea that he saw the moon flying on a windy night like a toy balloon. Do they think the moon can be moved by the wind? Focus on the lines *It's clouds that fly, and the moon and stars stand still in the sky*. Explain that the poet is using his imagination to describe what he saw.
● Go back to the way in which the poet likens the moon's 'movement' to that of a toy balloon (a simile). Ask the children for their own suggestions for describing movement in the wind. For example, how do the clouds look on a windy day? How do trees bend and move in the wind? Discuss the wind in different seasons.

Shared word-level work
● Ask the children to identify the rhymes in the poem: *night/white, balloon/moon, past/fast, fly and sky*. They may not initially recognise that *fly* and *sky* rhyme as *fly* doesn't appear at the end of a line, so re-read the poem to help them hear the rhymes.
● Through a quick brainstorm, reinforce the children's knowledge of *oo* words that have the same sound as *moon* and those that have the same sound as *good*.
● Recall words that rhyme with *fly* and make a list. Show the children that the *i* sound in *fly* can be written in different ways, for example *try, tie, high, by, buy*, and *bye*.
● Finally, ask for ideas for rhymes for *night* and *white*. (These appear in 'Narrative 2', so it might be helpful to refer to this if you have worked on the unit.)

Guided and independent work
● Work with a lower ability group to support their reading of 'Flying'. Discuss the content and help them to read with expression by modelling expressive reading and discussing its importance in engaging an audience's interest..
● Ask the children to work in pairs or small groups to find as many rhymes as they can for *moon, fly* and *night* and to make lists.
● Ask them to go on to write at least two lines for a poem about the moon on a windy night.

Differentiation

Less able
● Let children work with more able partners.

More able
● Encourage children to write at greater length and to prepare to perform their poems.

Plenary
● Share some of the children's lines from their poems with the rest of the group.
● Write *fly, night* and *moon* on the board and ask the children to suggest rhymes for each. Talk about the different ways in which the same sounds can be spelled and make three lists to use in the next lesson.
● Encourage the children to think of more rhymes for the three words and list them to bring to the next lesson. You could ask them to take this task home to look at with parents and carers.

UNIT 2 HOUR 9 Poetry

The moon on a windy night

Objectives

NLS
T12: To use simple poetry structures and to substitute own ideas, write new lines.
S4: To re-read own writing for sense and punctuation.
W4: To investigate and classify words with the same sounds but different spellings.

What you need
● Photocopiable page 33.

Shared text-level work
● Re-read 'Flying'. Explain to the children that you want them to use some of the rhyming words they found in the previous lesson, as well as some of the lines they wrote, to help you to write a poem about the moon on a windy night.
● Use the children's ideas and act as scribe, occasionally making deliberate errors and constantly saying aloud what you are doing and how you are revising the poem as you write it. Explain that the poem could follow a similar pattern to 'Flying', but encourage the children to discuss and decide upon the structure of the poem and to offer suggestions.
● When the poem has been written, ask the children to read it together and to offer ideas for revising and editing it. For example, would they replace some of they words with more descriptive language? Would they add metaphors or similes? Emphasise that revising and editing is an important part of writing, and that it enables us to improve quality and increase accuracy.
● Make changes to the poem and re-read it with the children, responding to their ideas for further revisions.

Shared word-level work
● Talk about the rhyming words again and refer to the three lists made in the previous lesson. Ask if anyone can think of words to add to the lists and include these, making a point of asking the children to spell the words aloud.

Guided and independent work
● Support the children as they continue their poems about the moon on a windy night. Encourage them to make use of ideas brought up in shared work.
● Ask yesterday's guided group to make collections of rhyming words while the rest of the class writes poems about the moon on a windy night. Encourage the children to draw upon the class lists to find rhymes and to help them to spell correctly.
● The guided group from the previous lesson could go on to write their own poems.
● Encourage all the children to re-read and revise their work independently and after showing it to and discussing it with partners.

Differentiation

Less able
● Children should work with more able classmates to produce their poems.

More able
● Ask children to use a word processor to write their poems and to import pictures to illustrate them.

Plenary
● Ask children to read their poems aloud. Discuss the content and the rhymes and address any spelling errors.
● Cover up the lists of rhyming words and say some of the words in sentences. Ask the children to write the words on their whiteboards and show what they have written.
● Check that the children understand that there are often different ways to spell the same sounds.

Objectives

NLS
T12: To use simple poetry structures and to substitute own ideas, write new lines.
S4: To re-read own writing for sense and punctuation.

S&L
15 Group discussion and interaction: To listen to each other's views and preferences.

What you need

● Photocopiable pages 32 and 33.

Evaluating the poems

Shared text-level work

● Remind the children about the poems they have read and the work they have done during the last two weeks.
● Show the four poems and read them together. Ask the children which poems they prefer and encourage them to justify their selections and to make reference to the texts.
● Talk about the different ways in which the poets describe the wind and its effects. Ask the children to discuss with their partners how the poets describe the sounds of the wind and any features they particularly like.
● Explain that they will be writing their own poems later and that they may use ideas from the poems to help them. They could either continue their poems from the previous day and polish and refine them or, if they are happy with them, they may write new ones.

Shared word- and sentence-level work

● Talk about the features of poems and rhymes in particular. Draw attention to the rhymes in the poems and remind the children about the different ways of writing some of the same phonemes.
● Ask them to tell you about the use of capital letters in poems. (Most have them at the beginning of each line.)

Guided and independent work

● Support the children in writing or continuing their poems. You may need to act as a scribe for some children to begin their lines of poetry, but encourage them to draw upon the word banks to complete them independently or in pairs.
● Ask children to make up or continue their own poems about the wind. Some may require a structure or framework, so write key words on the board, such as *wind, sky, clouds, trees, buildings, people.* Suggest that the children use one of the words in each line of their poems. Ask more able children to think about when their poem might be set – at what period of history and time of year. Suggest that they think about setting as well. They could set their poem in a different country or planet. Ensure that they adhere to the 'wind' theme.
● Display the collections of rhyming words to provide ideas to support their writing.

Differentiation

Less able
● Children could write their poems in note form and then receive adult help to write at greater length.

More able
● Ask children to prepare to perform their poems for the class when they have written them.

Plenary

● Share several of the poems and ask all the children to read their poems to partners.
● Note the children's understanding of the features of poetry and of the word- and sentence-level concepts they have developed in this unit. Address misconceptions and praise good quality work.
● As this is the last lesson in the unit, gather together copies of the children's poems and display them with the four poems they have read. Add photographs of wind and its effects as well as any artwork produced by the children.

Wind poetry (1)

The Wind

I can get through a doorway without any key,
And strip the leaves from the great oak tree.

I can drive storm clouds and shake tall towers,
Or steal through a garden and not wake the flowers.

Seas I can move and ships I can sink;
I can carry a house-top or the scent of a pink.

When I'm angry I can rave and riot;
And when I'm spent, I lie quiet as quiet.

James Reeves

Windy Nights

Whenever the moon and the stars are set,
  Whenever the wind is high,
All night long in the dark and wet,
  A man goes riding by.
Late in the night when the fires are out,
Why does he gallop and gallop about?

Whenever the trees are crying aloud,
  And the ships are tossed at sea,
By on the highway, low and loud,
  By at the gallop goes he.
By at the gallop he goes, and then
By he comes back at the gallop again.

Robert Louis Stevenson

Wind poetry (2)

Who Has Seen the Wind?

Who has seen the wind?
Neither I nor you;
But when the leaves hang trembling
The wind is passing through.

Who has seen the wind?
Neither you nor I;
But when the trees bow down their heads
The wind is passing by.

Christina Rossetti

Flying

I saw the moon
One windy night,
Flying so fast-
All silvery white-
Over the sky,
Like a toy balloon
Loose from its string-
A runaway moon.
The frosty stars
 Went racing past,
  Chasing her on
   Ever so fast.
    Then everyone said
     'It's clouds that fly, and the stars and moon
      stand still in the sky.'
       But I don't mind-
        I saw the moon
         Sailing away
          Like a toy
          Balloon.

JM Westrup

Word cards

Long vowel digraphs

room	cool	hoot	tool	tooth
moon	food	fool	brain	rain
train	main	snail	fail	paid
afraid	free	steel	deep	keep
peep	sleep	tree	feel	read
near	hear	bead	coat	boat
coal	goal	mouth	south	found
round				

'ou and 'ea'

you	sound	round	through	about
shout	four	pour	head	bread
seal	real	fear	near	ahead
ready	steady	dead	lead	lead
tea	near	would	should	easy
hear	meat	heat	read	read
found	ground			

'oo'

fool	pool	boot	zoo	book
too	roof	room	cook	tooth
spoon	foot	look	broom	wood
blood	soon	food	rook	balloon
tool	stood	cool	shoot	soot
shook	hook	wool		

Non-fiction 1: Instructions

This unit looks at different methods of presenting instructions. Children will study some of the different organisational devices used in instructions and will have the opportunity to engage in guided writing of instructions in a variety of forms. The unit is intended to precede the second unit on narrative, 'A walk in the dark woods'. Later in the term, it will be followed by a further instructions unit on instructions, decorating a Christmas tree.

Hour	Shared text-level work	Shared word-/ sentence-level work	Guided work	Independent work	Plenary
1 Doing as you are told	Reading diagram-based instructions and rewriting one set as sentences.	Discussing the different organisational devices in instructions.	Using oral instructions to begin writing simple instructions for each other	Writing instructions for each other, choosing different presentation models.	Discussing the children's instructions and picking out features.
2 Growing beans	Reading another simple set of instructions. Writing some in same format.	Discussing and practising use of capital letters.	Revise imperative verbs. Rewriting pictorial instructions in sentences.	Rewriting pictorial instructions in sentences.	Comparing features of instructions created.
3 Different types of instructions	Looking at different instructions for 'Hide and seek'.	Discuss language of time and words that link sentences. Revising imperative verbs.	Look at simple instructions and rewrite into sentences using language of time.	Working in groups to put a set of instructions into correct order. Using the language of time to write instructions.	Reviewing the children's sentences. Discussing language of time.
4 Underarm tig	Playing 'Underarm tig' then writing instructions on how to play the game.	Discussing organisational devices for instructions, including cyclical charts.	Writing instructions for tig, replacing full sentences with simple words or phrases.	Listing simple instructions for tig then making them into a cyclical diagram.	Comparing different methods of presenting instructions.
5 Writing instructions	Write instructions for another game of the children's choice and in their chosen format.	Discussing benefits of different organisational devices.	Writing instructions for chosen activity.	Writing instructions for chosen activity.	Following the instructions where possible.

Key assessment opportunities
- Can the children read simple instructions?
- Do they understand organisational features and use them in writing?
- Are they using capital letters correctly?
- Do they use the language of time to link sentences?

Doing as you are told

Objectives

NLS
T13: To read simple written instructions.
T14: To note key structural features, eg sequential steps.
S6: To use a variety of simple organisational devices to indicate sequences and relationships.

S&L
14 Listening: To listen to each other in class, ask relevant questions and follow instructions.

What you need
● Photocopiable page 41.

Shared text-level work
● Read the instructions with the children. Ask if they have seen similar instructions before and, if so, where.
● Focus on *Look>Say>Cover>Write>Check*. Point out that each instruction consists of one (imperative) verb that directly addresses the reader and that the sequence represents a strategy for learning the spelling of a word.
● With the children's help, expand each element into a short sentence, for example:

> Look at the word carefully.
> Say the word out loud.
> Cover the word.
> Write the word.
> Check that you have written the word correctly.

● Work with the children to write instructions on the board for a simple activity, such as cleaning teeth, eating an apple, in which each instruction consists only of one verb. The children should notice that it is often difficult to be precise without using nouns as well.

Shared sentence-level work
● Talk about the structural features of instructions, such as arrows, bullet points, numbers, picture sequences and sentences. Ask children to discuss in pairs which type of layout they find easiest to follow.
● Make up some simple instructions for the children. Write these on the board and ask them to follow them. For example, *Put your hands in the air. Fold your arms. Say hello to your partner.*
● Decide in which order the instructions should be presented and add arrows from one instruction to the next.

Guided and independent work
● Support the children in writing simple instructions for each other which feature imperative verbs and limited additional vocabulary. Make the activity more lively by beginning with oral instructions to be followed, as in a game like 'Simon says'. For example, instructions could include *Touch your shoulders. Put your hands on your head. Whisper to the person next to you.*
● Provide guidance on spellings and layout
● Organise the children to work in pairs to write simple instructions for each other. Each instruction could be one verb (*Smile, Laugh, Sing*), or short phrases and clauses (*Pull a face, Pick up your pencil*).
● Challenge children to produce as many different types of instructions as they can.

Differentiation

Less able
● Children may focus on oral instructions, but should be supported to produce at least one written instruction.

More able
● Ask children to produce sentences with two or more instructions, such as *Touch your nose with your right hand and your back with your left hand.*

Plenary
● Invite children to show and read their instructions for the others to follow. Discuss how clear and easy to follow they are.

Growing beans

Objectives

NLS
T16: To use models from reading to organise instructions sequentially.
S5: To revise knowledge about other uses of capitalisation, eg for names, headings, titles, emphasis, and begin to use in own writing.

What you need

● Recipe books and game instructions
● *Look>Say>Cover>Write> Check* from photocopiable page 41

Shared text-level work

● Explain to the children that you are going to show them instructions, written in short sentences, for an activity many of them will know well.
● Read and discuss the instructions for growing beans. Talk about the use of imperative verbs to begin lines, and show some examples from recipe books and game rules that use the same, simplified, abbreviated format.
● Ask the children to help you to write instructions using the same format, for example for making a drink, getting ready for playtime or writing a story.
● Move on to explain that you would like them to help you to rewrite the instructions in full sentences similar to those in the last lesson. Ask the children to remind each other about the features of these instructions.

Shared sentence-level work

● Make a point of talking about capital letters at the beginning of sentences as you write, and how you check your sentences to ensure there are no mistakes. By making some deliberate errors, you will encourage children to participate and they will enjoy correcting you!
● Ask the children to tell each other and then you some of the places where capital letters typically appear. They may talk about special names, titles and beginnings of sentences.

Guided and independent work

● Show the group the instructions for Look>Say>Cover>Write>Check. Remind them that in Hour 1 the class had developed these instructions into short sentences, each beginning with an imperative verb. Recall what the set of instructions is useful for and what each instruction means (*Look at the word, Say the word* and so on.)
● Ask the children to look at the pictorial instructions for eating a banana and then to write the instructions in sentences, using their own words and beginning each sentence with an imperative verb.
● Ask children to write instructions for Look>Say>Cover>Write>Check in complete sentences, each beginning with an imperative verb. They can adapt those from yesterday's session and use their own words, providing each sentence begins with *Look, Say, Cover, Write* and *Check* respectively.

Plenary

● Review the sentences the children have written, comparing different versions and noting features such as the use of imperative verbs.
● Talk about the use of capital letters to begin sentences, and ask children to tell each other and the class about other uses of capitals.
● Check whether the instructions could be followed easily. Discuss whether they are clear and simple, whether they could be followed, and if more information might be needed.

Differentiation

Less able
● Ask children to reproduce instructions pictorially with one or two words added to each picture.

More able
● Ask children to look at examples of instructions in books, including those in maths texts, and discuss features and language.

Different types of instructions

Objectives

NLS
T11: To use language of time to structure a sequence of events.
S2: To find examples of words and phrases that link sentences, eg *after*, *then*, *next*
W10: To learn new words from reading linked to particular topics.

S&L
15 Group discussion and interaction: To listen to each other's views and preferences, agree the next steps to take and identify contributions by each group member.

What you need
● Photocopiable pages 42 and 43.

Shared text-level work
● Look at the instructions for 'Hide and seek' and ask for comments on the ways in which they are presented.
● Ask the children if they can think of different ways of presenting the instructions, similar to those they saw in the last lesson.

Shared word- and sentence-level work
● Look at some of the sentences and discuss the ways in which they are presented differently, for example with numbers next to each instruction; with bullet points; with letters. Talk with the children about other ways in which instructions can be presented, such as diagrams, picture sequences and in writing with arrows between instructions.
● Note that items are separated and sequenced so that instructions may be followed step by step.
● Ask the children which instruction should be followed first, and then show them how we can use words and phrases such as *First, Next, Then, After that* and *Finally*, often at the beginning of sentences, to indicate a sequence.
● Point out that the verb comes after the sequence word. Look at each of the sentences and ask the children to identify the verbs. Ask them to discuss with partners other verbs which could be used in instructions for games (*pick, run, kick, take* and so on).

Guided and independent work
● Work with a lower ability group to look closely at the instructions for 'Hide and seek', and help them to rewrite the instructions using the language of time to link sentences and indicate a sequence.
● Discuss the meanings of the time words and encourage children to use Look>Say>Cover>Write>Check to learn their spellings.
● Ask children to read and cut out the jumbled instructions from photocopiable page 43 and arrange them in the correct order and, once they have checked, paste them onto paper. Explain that they should look at the time words at the beginnings of the sentences to help them to decide upon the correct order. Encourage them to work together and discuss and justify their choice.
● Now ask them to use the time words to write instructions for a different activity.

Plenary
● Ask the children to share their instructions for 'Hide and seek'. Discuss the vocabulary used and ask for constructive comments on the quality if the instructions.
● Check that they understand the use of time words to link sentences by asking where in a sequence they might expect to see sentences beginning with *First, Finally, Next* and *Then*.

Differentiation

Less able
● Ensure that there are capable readers on each table to help children to read the instructions.

More able
● Children may wish to add further time words and increase the number of instructions in their sequence.

Underarm tig

Objectives

NLS

T15: To write simple instructions, eg playing a game.

T17: To use diagrams in instructions, eg drawing and labelling diagrams as part of a set of instructions.

S6: To use a variety of simple organisational devices, eg arrows, lines, boxes, to indicate sequences.

W6: To read on sight high frequency words likely to occur in graded texts matched to the abilities of reading groups.

What you need

● Photocopiable page 44.

Shared text-level work

● Before the lesson, play 'Underarm tig'. The game can be played in the hall or playground or any restricted space large enough for children to run about safely.

● In the classroom, ask the children to give you instructions for the game and write these on the board. It doesn't matter if they don't give them in the correct order, as you can change them later.

Shared sentence-level work

● Show the children the flow diagram of the rules for 'Underarm tig' and ask them to compare it with the instructions they wrote with you.

● Talk about the use of a flow diagram to show a cycle of repeatable steps. Ask the children to show where the cycle begins and explain that the diagram is cyclical because the end of one game can become the start of another and so be played over and over again.

● Demonstrate that when instructions are presented in a diagram such as a flow chart it is not necessary to use the language of time to indicate a sequence.

● Look at some of the words in the instructions with the children to ensure that they can read and spell them, for example *person, everyone, someone.*

Guided writing

● Work with a lower ability group to discuss different ways in which the 'Tig' instructions could be presented. For example, they could use numbers, letters, bullet points or arrows.

● Help them to write the instructions simply, using single words, short phrases and clauses instead of sentences, so that they would be suitable for use in a flow diagram.

Independent work

● Ask children to produce instructions for 'Underarm tig' as a list.

● When they have done this, ask them to draw a cyclical diagram with sufficient boxes for their instructions to be copied into.

● Emphasise the importance of brief instructions in a diagram and explain that the sequential nature of the cyclical chart means that it is not necessary to use time language to precede instructions, except, perhaps, for the first instruction.

Differentiation

Less able

● Spend time showing children how to abbreviate the sentences.

More able

● Ask children to produce a non-cyclical flow chart for a different game.

Plenary

● Draw a blank cycle diagram on the board and ask for ideas for each instruction for an activity or game of their choice, for example tidying a drawer, getting ready for assembly. Begin by writing one child's idea and then improve this using suggestions from others.

● Explain to the children that they will be able to write instructions for their own choice of game or activity in the next lesson. They might wish to note down some ideas at home, discussing this with parents and carers.

Writing Instructions

Objectives

NLS

T15: To write simple instructions, eg getting to school, playing a game
T18 to use appropriate register in writing instructions, ie direct, impersonal, building on texts read.
S6: To use a variety of simple organisational devices, eg arrows, lines, boxes, keys, to indicate sequences and relationships.

What you need

● Photocopiable pages 42 and 44.

Shared text-level work

● Show children examples of instructions looked at in previous lessons to remind them of different ways of setting them out. Distribute photocopiable page 44 to remind the children of one potential layout for instructions for a game.
● Share ideas on activities and games for which they would like to produce instructions. Choose one idea and ask the class to help you to present it as a set of instructions, using whichever organisational device the children decide on.
● Having presented the instructions in one way, work to present them in another. For example, if you began with sentences, go on to produce a flow chart or cyclical diagram.

Shared sentence-level work

● Assess the different organisational devices and their features and what form may be the best for, for example, the rules of a game. Consider the need for them to be simple to understand and quick to read, but comprehensive. Should they be long or short? Is it important that they look attractive?
● Remind the children about the usefulness of numbered steps, bullet points, sequences of diagrams, and linking arrows.
● Using the different examples on photocopiable page 42, discuss instructions written in sentences or abbreviated phrases. Ask children to pick out imperative verbs and the language of time.

Guided and independent work

● Ask children to produce sets of instructions for their chosen activity or game. For those who have not prepared for this, offer suggestions for activities such as cleaning teeth, washing hair, getting dressed, painting a picture, playing noughts and crosses.
● Display photocopiable page 42, so that children may remind themselves of different forms of layout. Discuss the presentational methods and how to use them, and encourage children to choose their own preferred devices.
● Encourage children to work independently, but provide opportunities for them to discuss their work with others.

Differentiation

Less able

● Suggest children produce instructions in pictorial form, adding brief written notes with the help of others.

More able

● Ask children to use a computer to produce instructions and to experiment with different presentations.
● Encourage them to write instructions for a range of games.

Plenary

● Share the children's instructions. Initially, the children could do this in pairs, explaining how they presented the instructions and why they chose this layout.
● Where instructions are for a game that could safely be played in the classroom, ask some children to try out the game by reading and following the instructions.
● Show examples of board games with instructions. Assess how easy it is to follow those instructions. How clear are they? Is there any more detail that should have been added? Remind children that the more complicated the game is, the more complex its instructions.

Instructions

Look ➡ Say ➡ Cover ➡ Write ➡ Check

Growing Beans

Put soil in a plant pot.

⬇

Put seed in soil.

⬇

Water the soil.

⬇

Wait for plant to grow.

Eating a banana

1.

2.

3.

4.

TERM 1

Instructions for 'Hide and seek'

- First, choose one person to be the Finder.
- Next, tell the Finder to close his or her eyes and start counting to 50.
- Meanwhile everyone else quickly finds somewhere to hide.

NB. Never hide in a dangerous place. Keep out of wardrobes and cupboards because you might suffocate if someone closed the door.

- When the Finder has counted to 50, try to find the others.
- Finally, when everyone has been found, the first person to be found is the Finder for the next game.

A. Choose one person to be the Finder.
B. Tell the Finder to close his or her eyes and count to 50
C. Everyone else quickly go to hide.

NB. Never hide in a dangerous place. Keep out of wardrobes and cupboards because you might suffocate if someone closed the door.

D. The Finder must count to 50 and then try to find the others.
E. When everyone has been found, the first person to be found is the Finder for the next game.

1. CHOOSE A FINDER

2. FINDER CLOSES EYES AND COUNTS TO 50 WHILE EVERYONE HIDES (TAKE CARE!)

3. FINDER TRIES TO FIND OTHERS

4. FIRST TO BE FOUND IS THE NEXT FINDER

Jumbled instructions

Finally, when everyone has been found, the first person to be found is the Finder for the next game.

Next, tell the Finder to close his or her eyes and count to fifty while everyone else quickly hides.

Never hide in a dangerous place. Keep out of wardrobes and cupboards because you might suffocate if someone closed the door.

When the Finder has counted to 50 he or she should try to find the others.

First, choose one person to be the Finder.

Rules for 'Underarm tig'

1. Choose someone to be 'It'.

2. The person who is 'It' should count to ten. Everyone else should run away (It is best to have a rule that no one may leave a certain area, for example the playground or school hall.)

3. The person who is 'It' tries to catch the others and must tig them on their chest, arm or back.

4. When someone has been tigged they must stand still with their arms spread out until someone else goes under their arms to release them.

5. When everyone has been caught the last person to be caught is 'It' for the next game.

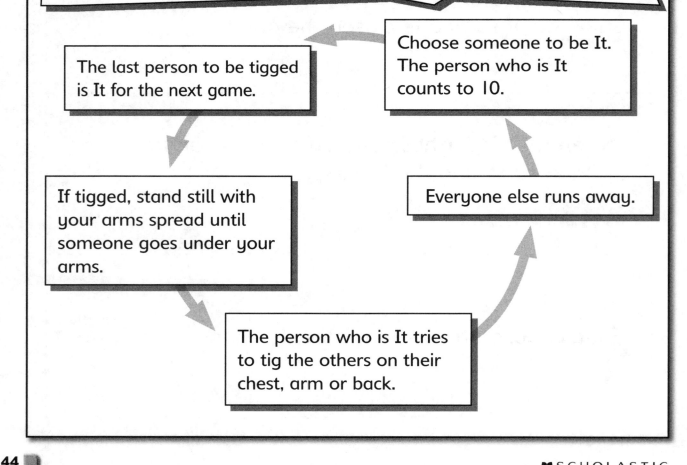

The last person to be tigged is It for the next game.

Choose someone to be It. The person who is It counts to 10.

If tigged, stand still with your arms spread until someone goes under your arms.

Everyone else runs away.

The person who is It tries to tig the others on their chest, arm or back.

UNIT 4 📄

Narrative 2

This 10-lesson unit is based on a four-part story about two children lost in the woods. In the fifth of each set of five days' lessons, there is an opportunity for extended writing that can continue beyond the Literacy Hour. Although the unit focuses on narrative, it includes a poem which describes night in the forest, which can be used to provide children with further ideas for their own writing. This unit also covers *Developing early writing,* unit A. and *Progression in phonics,* step 7.

Hour	Shared text-level work	Shared word-/ sentence-level work	Guided work	Independent work	Plenary
1 Lost! 💬	Reading the story and considering the theme.	Using grammar to decipher unfamiliar words.	Identifying unfamiliar words, learning to spell them and using them in sentences.	Asking classmates about unfamiliar words. Identifying words that still need to be learned.	Looking at unfamiliar words and at *-ed, -ing* and *-s* endings.
2 What happens next?	Re-reading part 1 of the story. Discussing story structure. Speculating on what might happen next.	Revise knowledge about capitalisation.	Planning the next part of the story Writing sentences or dialogue.	Planning the next part of the story Writing sentences or dialogue.	Looking at examples of children's writing, discussing structure and use of capital letters.
3 Voices in the woods	Reading the second part of the story. Comparing it with the children's plans. Discussing story theme.	Looking at selection of words from the text and identifying phonemes and blending phonemes.	Guided re-reading of the text and discussion of phonemes.	Building words from initial sounds, medial sounds and final sounds.	Segmenting and building more words.
4 What's missing? 💬	Re-reading the story with some words missing. Predicting words and meanings.	Using grammar to decipher unfamiliar words.	Predicting missing words. Inventing own cloze sentences.	Discussing missing words in pairs.	Discussing different ideas for missing words.
5 Still lost!	Beginning to retell the story.	Looking at long vowel sounds and different ways in which these can be written.	Planning and rewriting part of the story. Revising long-vowel phonemes.	Using cloze exercise as springboard for retelling.	Looking at children's stories and discussing spellings of words with long vowel sounds.

UNIT 4

Hour	Shared text level work	Shared word/ sentence level work	Guided work	Independent work	Plenary
6 Timeless	Reading 'Timeless'. Analysing descriptions of night in the forest.	Look at rhyming words and at spellings of different long vowel sounds, eg *white, bright*.	Reading with expression and intonation.	Writing rhyming couplets with same setting as 'Timeless'.	Reading couplets aloud. Noting any words rhyming with *night*.
7 In the past	Reading part 3 of the story. Discussing using punctuation when reading dialogue aloud. Speculating what might happen next.	Using actions to demonstrate words ending with *-ed*.	Writing rhyming couplets with same setting as 'Timeless'.	Changing sentences from present to past tense by using *-ed* ending.	Reading aloud. Noting *-ed* endings and punctuation.
8 Found!	Reading the story ending. Discussing about story structure.	Identifying use of commas in the text and re-reading, taking them into account.	Preparing dramatic reading of the text.	Punctuating sentences.	Putting commas into sentences. Watching dramatised reading.
9 Planning a story	Developing a story plan about getting lost.	Spelling key words for their plans. Segmenting words into phonemes.	Preparing a plan for a story.	Preparing a plan for a story.	Talking about plans, including characters and settings. Adding to word bank.
10 Writing a story	Writing story opening, using children's plans.	Re-reading of paragraph to check for sense and punctuation. Revising key words.	Extended writing using plans for story.	Extended writing using plans for story.	Sharing children's work and discussing story structure.

Key assessment opportunities
● Can the children identify themes and sequences of events?
● Do they segment and blend phonemes when reading and spelling?
● Do they use capital letters and commas correctly?
● Do they understand the *-ed* ending changes verbs from present to past tense?
● Can they use grammar and context to predict unfamiliar words?

Lost!

Objectives

NLS
T6: To discuss familiar story themes and link to own experiences.
S1: To use awareness of grammar to decipher new or unfamiliar words.
W7: To use word endings, eg 's' (plural), 'ed' (past tense), 'ing' (present tense) to support their reading and spelling.

S&L
14 Listening: To listen to others in class, ask relevant questions and follow instructions.

What you need
● Photocopiable page 57
● dictionaries.

Shared text-level work
● Show the text to the children and ask them about the title. What does it make them think about?
● Read the text and ask the children how the story makes them feel. Can they imagine themselves in a similar situation? What would they do if they were lost? What do they think David and Imran should do?

Shared word- and sentence-level work
● Point to some of the less familiar words in the text and ask the children if they know what they mean. Show them how to use the surrounding words and context to work out meanings.
● Read out some of the sentences, pausing at unfamiliar words. Then ask the children to tell you about the word and what it does. Does it tell the reader how someone spoke? Does it describe something? Ask the children to guess what the word might be and discuss whether their guess is good, in that the word could make sense in the context. Where appropriate, you could use the word ending (-s, -ed, -ing) as a clue.
● Discuss the use of -s, -ed and -ing to modify words, and ask the children to suggest examples.

Guided and independent work
● Identify less familiar words in the text. Discuss the words and ask the children to write their own sentences that include them.
● Help the children with their spellings, and use the opportunity to focus on word endings such as -ed, -ing and -s.
● Ask children to work in pairs to discuss and list unfamiliar words. After ten minutes or so, ask them to share their lists with another pair and help each other by explaining any words they know. Encourage them to ask each other questions.
● Ask each group of four to produce a list of words that no one can define or read to bring to the plenary session.
● If time permits, encourage them to write some of the new words in sentences.

Plenary
● Discuss the words that children either cannot read or cannot define. Write these on the board, asking the children to read them aloud after you. Look at the correspondence between phonemes and graphemes.
● Revise dictionary use with the children. Ask them to use the dictionary to look for definitions of unfamiliar words, reminding them that the dictionary is organised alphabetically.
● Ask children to help you to write the words in sentences, focusing on the spellings of -ed, -ing and -s endings.
● Try writing some sentences in which a word needs s, ed or ing to be added in order for it to be grammatically correct. For example: *I ate three apple; I walk to school yesterday; I am talk to my friend on the phone at the moment.*

Differentiation

Less able
● Encourage children to ask more able readers to explain some of the words.

More able
● Ask children to go on to look at further words. They should say incomplete sentences and ask others to complete them by choosing from the words.

UNIT 4 HOUR 2 📖 Narrative 2

What happens next?

Objectives

NLS
T4: To understand time and sequential relationships in stories, ie what happened when.
S5: To revise knowledge about other uses of capitalisation, eg for names, headings, titles, and begin to use in own writing.

What you need
● Photocopiable page 57.

Shared text-level work
● Show the children the first part of the story again and discuss the events so far. Focus on story structure and talk about a beginning, a middle and an ending.
● Explain that this part of the story is the beginning and so it needs to gain readers' attentions quickly and make them want to read on. For example, the story begins with a short question that is *hissed* by Imran. Immediately, the reader wonders what is happening.
● With the children's help, pick out the key events in the first part of the story, for example:

1. Boys hear sounds.
2. They look for the adults.
3. They become frightened.
4. They can't find Imran's parents.
5. They listen but can only hear the wind and an owl.

● Show how these brief notes can use only one or two words to represent a whole sentence or event.
● Ask the children what they think might happen next in the story and to explain their ideas by making reference to the text.

Shared sentence-level work
● Using the children's ideas, write the first two sentences of the next part of the story.
● Comment on the use of capital letters to begin sentences and for proper nouns. Cite some examples from the story: ask why *David* and *Imran* always have initial capitals and why *the* has no capital in the second sentence, but has one at the beginning of the second paragraph.

Guided and independent work
● Ask the children to work in pairs to write outlines for the first part of the story, then discuss what might happen next. From this discussion, they should make a plan for the next part of the story.
● When they have finished, ask them to write at least one sentence that they think could begin the second part of the story. Encourage them to think carefully about where they place capital letters, and check that they understand that all sentences and names begin with capitals.

Differentiation

Less able
● Talk with children again about the first part of the story and support them as they produce outlines of the story opening.

More able
● Ask children to continue writing the second part of the story.

Plenary
● Look at examples of the children's plans and sentences. Identify the uses of capital letters.
● Write some of the children's sentences on the board, deliberately leaving out the capitals, and ask the authors to check that you have written their sentences correctly.

Voices in the woods

Objectives

NLS
T2: To use phonological, contextual, grammatical and graphic knowledge to work out, predict and check the meanings of unfamiliar words and to make sense of what they read.
W3: To identify phonemes in speech and writing; to blend phonemes for reading; to segment the words into phonemes for spelling.

What you need
● Photocopiable page 58
● enlarged copies of some of the children's opening sentences from Hour 2
● simple dictionaries for each table and one more advanced dictionary.

Differentiation

Less able
● Encourage children to make their words orally, with adult or more able children scribing.

More able
● Challenge children to make the longest word they can with as many of the graphemes as possible.

Shared text-level work
● Look again at the children's sentences and explain that you are now going to show them the next part of the story. Compare the children's ideas with those in the text. The first two lines are dialogue. Did anyone choose to begin in this way?
● Read part 2 and discuss how David and Imran feel? Why did a twig crack? Who could the voices belong to?

Shared word-level work
● Talk about some of the words in the story that have three parts, for example an initial consonant-consonant blend or digraph followed by a medial vowel or familiar vowel digraph and then a final consonant-consonant blend or digraph. These could include: *trick, trees, twig, wind, sound, help, cross, stood, think* and *hear.*
● Demonstrate how the words can be broken down into three sound-parts. Model blending the phonemes, taking care to avoid adding an additional vowel sound (for example, when sounding *trick,* avoid tru-i-cku, *sum* should be sounded as ss-u-mm rather than as su-u-mu).
● Write examples of single sounds, digraphs and blends in three columns on the board. For example:

| sh | a | i | o | ck | ss | sh | b. | tr | bl | cr |

● Ask volunteers to take turns to choose a sound from each column and to make a word from the three parts, for example *track.*

Guided and independent work
● Work with a group to guide their reading of part 2 of the story. Look at some of the difficult words they encounter and discuss ways of sounding them by segmenting them into phonemes.
● Write difficult words on a large sheet of paper and discuss them again at the end of the session
● As independent work, ask the children to use the graphemes in the three columns to build as many words as they can. Provide simple dictionaries so that children can check to see if their words exist. Explain that they may produce some words that don't appear in a simple dictionary, but that you will help them to check these from a larger dictionary at the end of the lesson.

Plenary
● Write on the board some of the words the children have created and ask everyone to break them into phonemes and blend them.
● Check on any real words that might not be in the simple dictionaries, for example, *crick, trash* and *crass.*
● Write some new examples on the board.

🔲 **49**

What's missing?

Objectives

NLS
T2: To use phonological, contextual, grammatical and graphic knowledge to work out, predict and check the meanings of unfamiliar words and to make sense of what they read.
S1: To use awareness of grammar to decipher new or unfamiliar words, eg to predict from the text; to read on, leave a gap and re-read.

S&L
15 Group discussion and interaction: To listen to each other's views and preferences, agree the next steps to take and identify contributions by each group member.

What you need
● Cloze version of photocopiable page 58 (cover at least one word per sentence)
● photocopiable page 61.

Shared text-level work
● Show the children the cloze version of part 2 of the story. Explain that they will probably be able to work out the missing words because they have read the text before, so you want them to listen carefully and think about what each missing word might be.
● Read the text and pause slightly or say *Mmm* when you come to a missing word. Read to the end before asking children to listen again and suggest what the missing word might be as you read to the end of each sentence.
● Make it clear that, although there is a 'correct' word for each space – the one from the original text – the children are not 'wrong' if they suggest a word that fits equally well. For example, for the sentence *David said, 'I think we should get out of the woods and find ___.'* Children might reasonably suggest: *help, them* or *safety*. Make it clear that each space represents only one word.

Shared sentence-level work
● Talk about using semantic and grammatical clues, in conjunction with phonic clues, to help decipher unfamiliar words. Emphasise the importance of reading to the end of a sentence and then re-reading before deciding what a word might be.
● Try writing some cloze sentences, for example *The dog ___ after the car*, then putting inappropriate words in the spaces. Ask the children to explain why the words do not fit. Try reading the sentence with a noun, adjective or preposition in the space, before asking for suggestions for appropriate verbs.

Guided and independent work
● Work with a group to complete photocopiable page 61.
● Then ask them to make up their own cloze sentences so that the group can suggest and discuss words that would fit.
● Provide photocopiable page 61 for each pair of children. Encourage them to discuss their ideas first, and remind them that there may be several words that could fit. Where the children agree that there could be more than one word that would fill a space, tell them to write their preferred choice, but put an asterisk next to it and write the other word in the margin, for example *or them*.

Differentiation

Less able
● Encourage children to contribute their ideas orally.

More able
● Ask children to go on write their own cloze sentences for their partners to complete.

Plenary
● Work through photocopiable 61 and discuss the suggestions made by the children, especially where alternatives have been given. Discuss the relative merits of the children's suggestions and ask them to talk about which they prefer.
● Emphasise the importance of reading on and re-reading, and of using the sense of the sentence to help them to make appropriate suggestions.
● Ask children to come up with as many different words as possible that would make sense in a cloze sentence.

Still lost!

Objectives

NLS
T5: To identify and discuss reasons for events in stories, linked to plot.
S4: To re-read own writing for sense and punctuation.
W1: To secure identification, spelling and reading of long vowel digraphs in simple words from Y1 term 3.

What you need
● Photocopiable page 58
● completed photocopiable page 61
● tape recorders.

Shared text- and sentence-level work
● Recall part 2 of the story with the children and list the key events on the board. Explain that this will form a plan for use in retelling the story.
● Ask the children to help you to begin writing this part of the story, using only the plan. Discuss the key points in the second part of the story. Why do they think the boys are becoming anxious? What was the noise they heard? What had Imran's parents always told him?
● As you write, occasionally make deliberate errors such as omitting capital letters or misspelling simple words, and encourage the children to spot the errors and correct them. Re-read as you incorporate the corrections. Remind the children of the importance of re-reading their work, not only to check for errors, but to improve the style and content and make the work more descriptive.

Shared word-level work
● Pick out any words from the shared writing that have long vowel sounds and ask the children to suggest words with similar sounds. Write these on the board and show that they can be classified according to their spelling. For example, in part 2 *they, away* and *made* all have the same long vowel sound but each is spelled differently.
● Discuss examples of split vowel digraphs with the children (for example, t*a*ke, s*i*de, n*o*te, t*u*be) and ask them to suggest further examples.

Guided and independent work
● Support one group's rewriting of the second part of the story. Begin by asking them to make a brief plan of events and ask them to use these as a framework for their writing. Explain that they will be given additional time to complete their stories after the Literacy Hour if necessary, so they do not need to rush.
● Stop them occasionally to discuss their work and to focus on spelling and the use of capital letters. In particular, look for examples of words that have long vowel sounds. Confirm their spellings.
● Ask children to use their completed cloze exercises as prompts to help them to structure their writing of the second part of the story. Explain that they should not copy from the story, but may re-read it to remind them of what happened.
● Encourage children to re-read their work for sense and to check for correct usage of capital letters and full stops. They should also check for correct spellings of words written on the board earlier.

Differentiation

Less able
● Some children could tape record their stories to be typed up later.

More able
● Children should be encouraged to draft, edit and revise their work and to use dictionaries to check spellings.

Plenary
● Read out some of the children's stories and discuss the content. Focus on spellings of words with long vowel sounds and write examples from the children's stories on the board.
● Follow up by producing lists of words with the long vowel sounds from the NLS Appendix List 3. These can be added to as the children learn new words. Display these lists in the classroom.

Timeless

Objectives

NLS
T7: To re-read and recite favourite poems, taking account of punctuation; to comment on aspects such as word combinations, sound patterns (such as rhymes, rhythms, alliterative patterns) and forms of presentation.
W4: To investigate and classify words with the same sounds but different spellings.

What you need
● Photocopiable page 62.

Shared text-level work
● Ask the children where and when the story they have been reading is set. (In the woods and in the dark – at night.)
● Read Judith Nicholls' poem and explain that she is describing night-time in a forest.
● Discuss this description in more detail. Nicholls suggests that there is no clock in the forest but we can tell the time by the things that happen there, such as the owl hunting when light has gone, a mouse sleeping until night comes, the pale light of dawn, and the stars disappearing.
● Re-read the poem with the children and discuss the way it is presented almost like a list. Ask them to try to identify the rhymes in the poem. The poem has only one pair of rhyming lines in the first verse, where *blow* in the second line rhymes with *below* in the seventh, while the second verse has lines 3, 5 and 7 rhyming.

Shared word-level work
● Talk about the rhyming of long vowel sounds in *blow* and *below*, and *white, bright* and *light*. Ask the children to suggest more words that rhyme with these, and list them on the board.
● Many of the words children will know that rhyme with white will end with *-ight*, for example, *night, tight, fight* and *right*. If the children cannot think of many words spelled *-ite*, suggest some to get them started: *write, site, bite, invite, excite*.
● Add some of the words to the displayed lists of words with long vowel sounds (see the plenary in Hour 5).

Guided and independent work
● Support a group as they write rhyming couplets about night-time in the forest. Ask them to use simple sentences, one of which should end with *night*.
● Help them to produce sentences that rhyme by brainstorming rhyming words and writing phrases on a large piece of paper so that all the group can see it.
● Ask children to write simple sentences that combine to describe night time in the forest. Advise them to end their first sentence with *night*, and to use this as a starting point for producing a simple rhyme.
● Ask them to go on to produce further rhyming couplets about night in the forest.

Differentiation

Less able
● Provide children with pairs of rhyming words to use in their couplets.

More able
● Challenge children to write at greater length and to prepare to read their poems to the class.

Plenary
● Ask children to read their couplets aloud. Write some of the couplets on the board and discuss the images created.
● Focus on words that rhyme with *night*, and add any new ones to the long vowel sound lists.
● Discuss different ways in which the same sound can be written and ask the children to suggest examples for you to write on the board.
● Introduce children to more poetry that is in different forms, such as shape poems, kennings and limericks.

In the past

Objectives

NLS
S3: To recognise and take account of commas and exclamation marks in reading aloud with appropriate expression.
W7: To use word endings, eg *ed* (past tense), to support their reading and spelling.

S&L
13 Speaking: To speak with clarity and use intonation when reading and reciting texts.

What you need
● Photocopiable page 59.

Differentiation

Less able
● Ensure that children have more able partners to work with.

More able
● Ask children to write further dialogue for the story. For example, a conversation between the boys and the police. Remind them about punctuation marks in dialogue.

Shared text- and sentence-level work
● Read the third part of the story to the children.
● Re-read, asking three children to read the parts of the policeman, policewoman and Imran, with the rest of the class reading the rest of the text. Talk about the importance of speaking clearly and expressively so that others can hear and understand. Emphasise the importance of pausing at commas, and discuss the effect the exclamation marks should have on the way the words are spoken.
● Recall the sequence of events that led up to this part of the story and discuss what might happen next.

Shared word-level work
● Talk about some of the words in the text that end with -*ed*. Explain that this ending shows that something has already happened. See if the children can give the present and past tense versions of the words. This may best be done through actions. For example, ask certain children to jump, shout, grab or mutter by saying, *Please jump now* and so on. Then ask the rest of the class what the child just did. Ask them to answer in sentences, such as *Mark jumped up and down* and *Rebecca shouted at the top of her voice*. Explain to the children that we use past tense for things that have just happened, and also for things that happened a long time ago. For example, we might say *The Battle of Hastings happened in 1066* and *The school fair happened last week*, and we must use our judgement to tell the difference between the two.
● Now show the children how to write the sentences, paying particular attention to adding -*ed* to the root word.

Guided and independent work
● Work with a group of more able children to read part 3 of the story. Help them to adopt roles and read with appropriate expression and intonation in preparation for reading to the class during the plenary.
● On the board write the words *hoot, call, shout, ask* and *grab*. Ask the children to work in pairs to write at least one sentence for each word, in the past tense. Before they begin, point out that when *grab* becomes *grabbed* it has a double b, but each of the other words simply adds -*ed*. The children could write simple sentences, with the more able writing dialogue.

Plenary
● Ask children to read out some of their sentences aloud. Write some examples on the board and discuss the use of -*ed* endings and, for those who have written dialogue, any use of commas, question marks and exclamation marks.
● Ask the guided group to read the story. Ask other to comment on their use of expression and intonation, and encourage children to read the story aloud in small groups after discussing ways in which this might be done. Ask some groups to read to the class.

UNIT 4 HOUR 8 ⬛ Narrative 2

Found!

Objectives
NLS
T6: To discuss familiar story themes.
S3: To recognise and take account of commas and exclamation marks in reading aloud with appropriate expression.

S&L
16 Drama: To adopt appropriate roles in small or large groups.

What you need
● Photocopiable pages 58–60
● Unpunctuated sentences related to the story (see Guided and independent work).

Differentiation

Less able
● Encourage children to read the sentences aloud before attempting punctuation.

More able
● Ask children to write sentences of their own which include commas and perhaps speech marks.

Shared text-level work
● Revise parts 1 to 3 of the story. Explain to the children that they are going to read the final part of the story, but first ask them to talk in pairs, to recall the events so far and to discuss how they think it might end.
● Read part 4.
● Talk about how the story ends and discuss other adventure or scary stories they know that have happy endings. Ask them if they like the ending. Would they have liked the story to have ended differently? Can they suggest alternative endings?
● Re-read part of the story, for example from the fifth paragraph, and ask the children to listen carefully and tell you when you have finished what a reader should do when s/he reaches a comma. (Pause slightly.)

Shared sentence-level work
● Develop this discussion of commas. Ask the children if they can tell you some uses of commas, for example in lists and just before closing speech marks when followed by a verb and the name of the speaker.
● With the children's help, write a variety of different types of sentences that should include commas, discussing where commas ought to be placed and why.

Guided and independent work
● As guided work, ask the children to re-read part 4 as a group. Ask them to read different parts aloud with different members of the group having different roles. Encourage the children to discuss the roles and to agree who will do what. Some children could read the dialogue for different characters, while others read the prose.
● Look for signs that they understand that they need to pause slightly when they reach a comma. Help them to prepare to read the story ending to the class in the plenary.
● Provide some unpunctuated sentences for the children to read and then punctuate. These can be written on the board and should be related to the story. The focus is on commas, but full stops and question marks should be included too. The sentences could include:
PC Parker WPC Scott David and Imran went to meet Imran's parents
Mr Khan Mrs Khan David and Imran walked back to the caravan
We'll have some hot chocolate said Mrs Khan
Would you like some chocolate biscuits asked Mr Khan

Plenary
● Look at the sentences on the board with the whole class and ask children to help you to punctuate them.
● Ask the guided group to present their dramatised reading. Use this to begin discussion about different text types – how stories, plays and poems differ. Discuss with the class the way in which we can use the punctuation to help them to read with appropriate intonation and expression.

Objectives

NLS
T4: To understand time and sequential relationships in stories, ie what happened when.
T10: To use story structure to write about own experience in same/similar form.
W3: To segment the words into phonemes for spelling.

Planning a story

Shared text-level work
● Recall the story of David and Imran getting lost in the woods and explain to the children that they are going to write their own stories about getting lost. First, they need to plan their stories.
● Discuss the features of a plan and remind them about the plans made in Hours 2 and 5. Explain that these should be brief and often in note form, should be sequential for a story and should indicate the setting and the characters involved.
● With the children's help, write a plan for a story about getting lost. Draw upon the children's ideas by brainstorming with the class and jotting their ideas on the board. Talk about setting, characters, and plot and write brief notes for each event in the story.

Shared word-level work
● Go over the spellings of difficult but useful words that may come up in the plan. Show how they can be segmented into phonemes and help the children understand the match between phonemes and graphemes. Draw attention to long vowel phonemes in particular.
● Display the words so that the children can refer to them whenever necessary, and add them to spelling logs.

Guided and independent work
● Ask children to plan their stories. Remind them that the plan should help them to structure the story with a beginning, a middle, and an ending. Ask them to word their plans succinctly and set them out sequentially, making sure that their story flows well and that they use plenty of linking words. Remind them of the importance of detailing the setting, and noting when the setting changes.
● Make notes on interesting, descriptive words for settings so that the children can write more atmospheric stories.
● Encourage them to share their ideas in pairs.
● Ask them to think about the story characters and to give them names, remembering that these must begin with capital letters.
● Support a middle ability group as they plan stories in pairs. Suggest that they use organisational devices encountered when writing instructions, such as arrows, lines and boxes.
● Encourage the children to discuss their ideas and make suggestions to each other about the content of their stories.

Differentiation

Less able
● Children should work with more able partners.

More able
● Ask children to use word processors to plan their stories, encouraging them to save their notes so that they can cut and paste them when they expand them into a story.

Plenary
● Discuss the plans and ask some of the children to tell you about the stories they are going to write. Talk about the importance of characters and settings as well as plot. Discuss the sequence in which events can be presented in a story, and talk about interesting ways in which to begin a story so that the reader's interest is engaged.
● Add to the word bank by drawing upon the vocabulary in the children's plans. Practise spellings and phoneme/grapheme correspondence.

UNIT 4 HOUR 10 📖 Narrative 2

Writing a story

Objectives

NLS

T11: To use language of time to structure a sequence of events.
S4: To re-read own writing for sense and punctuation.

S&L
14 Listening: To listen to others in class, ask relevant questions and follow instructions.

Shared text- and sentence-level work

● Explain to the children that in this final lesson they will be undertaking extended writing. Remind them that they will be using their plans to write a story about getting lost.

● Talk about story openings and ask one child to tell the class about how his or her story will begin. Write an opening sentence and discuss it with the children. Can they suggest ways in which it could be improved? Does it make the reader want to read on?

● Continue to develop the opening until you reach the 'middle' section of the child's plan.

● Then read what you have written and again, ask for suggestions for improvements if appropriate.

● Recap some of the words and phrases that children could use to help them to sequence events and link sentences, for example, *suddenly, then, after a while, meanwhile.*

● Talk about the importance of reading work through to check that it makes sense and that others may enjoy it. Emphasise that when they write their stories you would like them to focus on the content and that they should not worry too much about spellings at first. However, they should re-read and check their work before showing it to anyone else. It is at this stage that accuracy is most important so that other people can understand what they have written.

Guided and independent work

● Ask the children to use their plans to help them to write a story. Ask them to select the ideas they like best from their plan, but also to add new ideas they or others in their group might have.

● Encourage them to talk about their stories and to share ideas and discuss ways in which they might write sentences and sequence events. Ask them to listen carefully to what others say about their stories and to act upon advice where appropriate. Encourage them to ask for advice, try out ideas and offer constructive suggestions to each other without being too critical.

● Work with different groups during a longer than usual writing session and stop the class occasionally to share interesting phrases and sentences.

Differentiation

Less able
● Help children to get started by discussing story openings and sequences of events.

More able
● Children who were planning their stories on computer should use them again to develop the plans into stories.

Plenary

● There won't be time to read all of the stories, so allow children to share their stories in small groups and then ask them to tell you about the good ideas their classmates had. Encourage children to share their ideas for developing and improving each other's stories. Emphasise that their suggestions should be constructive.

● Follow up the activity by allowing children to complete their stories and make final copies for display on the wall or in a class book about getting lost.

● Discuss how people feel when they are lost and what we can do to help them.

A walk in the dark woods – part 1

"What was that?" whispered Imran.

"What was what?" replied David quietly, looking around him at the dark trees that surrounded them.

"That rustling sound, continued Imran nervously. "It came from over there. I think we're being followed."

"It's probably a bird, or a mouse or something," said David. "Come on, let's catch up with your parents before we get lost."

The boys hurried along the muddy path that led them deeper into the dark woods. Imran's parents had told them it would be a great idea to walk together in the woods after dark, because they would be able to hear owls and nightjars and might even see a bat. Imran, who didn't like the dark at all, would rather have been in the cosy caravan playing games or watching television, but Mr Khan had insisted that they all go for a walk after tea.

Suddenly, David stopped and turned to Imran with a frightened look on his face. Imran, who had been following very close behind David, stumbled into him and nearly fell.

"Oy! What are you doing?" he cried.

"I can't see your mum and dad anywhere," mumbled David. "I think we're lost!"

Mrs Khan had told the boys to keep close to them in the woods and not wander off on their own. They had meant to keep up with the grown ups, but when Imran caught sight of a rabbit and persuaded David to look for a rabbit hole, they had been left behind.

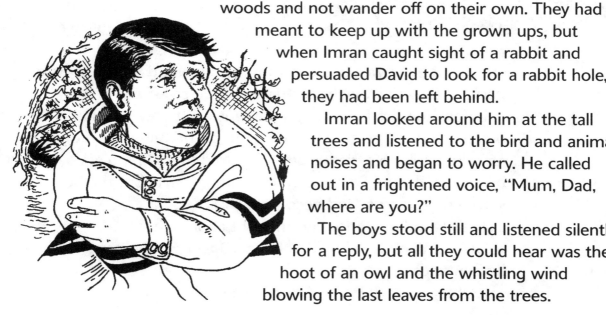

Imran looked around him at the tall trees and listened to the bird and animal noises and began to worry. He called out in a frightened voice, "Mum, Dad, where are you?"

The boys stood still and listened silently for a reply, but all they could hear was the hoot of an owl and the whistling wind blowing the last leaves from the trees.

TERM 1

A walk in the dark woods – part 2

"They must be playing a trick on us," said Imran.

"Yeah, they're probably hiding in the trees, watching us," whispered David. The boys looked around at the trees to see if anything or anyone was moving. There was a sudden cracking of a twig a few metres away and both boys jumped.

"They're over there," cried David, but when they peered into the darkness they couldn't see anyone.

"Mum, Dad, we know you're there. Come out now please," called Imran. But there was no reply. Only the wind and the night birds made any sound at all.

"They're not there," whispered David. "If they were, they would have answered. I'm worried. I think we should get out of the woods and find help. Perhaps they think we're lost and they've called the police."

Imran stood still and thought about what they should do. His parents had always told him never to go off on his own or to go anywhere with his friends unless he told them first. They would be cross if he and David went off on their own, but the boys were on their own, and becoming afraid.

They stood in silence and thought about what to do.

"Well, I think we should..." began David. But he never finished his sentence.

"Shhhh!" hissed Imran. I think I can hear voices.

A walk in the dark woods – part 3

"Got you!" shouted a deep voice.

Imran and David jumped and then grabbed at each other's arms.

Out of the darkness loomed a tall, dark figure holding a torch.

From the other side of the path another figure appeared, smaller but still dark and shadowy.

"Stay where you are! It's alright, we won't hurt you," said a softer, female voice.

"Are you David and Imran?" asked the deep voice as the two figures came nearer.

"Y-y-y-es," muttered Imran nervously.

"We thought as much," said the woman. "Now just stay where you are. There's nothing to be afraid of. I'm WPC Scott and this is PC Parker. We met your parents in the woods and they asked us to help them look for you."

A walk in the dark woods – part 4

The boys had both thought of running away, but the woman's voice was kind and suddenly they didn't feel afraid any more.

The police stood close to the boys and shone their torches towards themselves as they showed their police cards with their names on. The cards had photographs and PC Parker and WPC Scott shone their torches so the boys could see that their faces matched the photographs.

"Come on, let's go and find your parents, Imran. They're very worried," said PC Parker and he took Imran's hand while WPC Scott took David's.

It only took a few minutes to get to the edge of the wood where Mr and Mrs Khan were waiting anxiously. Mrs Khan ran to Imran and put her arms around him and kissed him on the cheek. "Thank goodness you're safe," she cried.

"Mum, stop it, you're embarrassing me!" said Imran, but secretly he was glad to be hugged by his mother because, a few minutes earlier, he had thought he might not see her again.

Mr Khan ruffled David's hair and put his arm around his shoulder.

"I'm so glad you're both safe," he said. "Please don't ever make us worry like that again."

Mr and Mrs Khan thanked the police for their help, and then they walked back to the caravan with the boys, who kept very close to them and didn't take their eyes off them even for a moment.

"Let's have some nice hot chocolate and you two can tell us what you've been up to," said Mrs Khan.

"And I think some chocolate biscuits might help them to remember, don't you?" laughed Mr Khan.

Part 2 summary

■ Fill in the missing words.

Imran thought his parents might be playing a _____ on the boys.

The boys _____ when they heard a _____ crack.

The only sounds in the dark woods were the _____ and the night _____

Imran's friend was called _____ .

David said, "I think we should get out of the woods and find _____ ."

Imran's _____ told him _____ to go anywhere without telling them first.

_____ thought he heard voices.

Timeless

There is no clock in the forest
but a dandelion to blow,
an owl that hunts
when the light has gone,
a mouse that sleeps
till night has come,
lost in the moss below.

There is no clock in the forest,
only the cuckoo's song
and the thin white
of the early dawn,
the pale damp-bright
of a waking June,
the bluebell light
of a day half-born
when the stars have gone.

There is no clock in the forest.

Judith Nicholls

UNIT 5

Non-fiction 2: Instructions

This non-fiction unit on instructions is designed to take place towards the end of term and after, though not necessarily immediately after, children have worked on the 'Non-fiction 1: Instructions' activities. Children will explore other organisational devices, and their understanding of sequential organisation and the appropriate register for instructions will be developed. The first four lessons involve looking at diagrams and sentences, while the fifth lesson provides children with the opportunity to produce their own instructions for an activity of their choice.

Hour	Shared text-level work	Shared word-/ sentence-level work	Guided work	Independent work	Plenary
1 Decorating the tree	Looking at a diagram of a decorated Christmas tree. Using the labels in sentences.	Establishing spellings of unfamiliar words.	Write key words in sentences in instructions format.	Write key words in sentences in instructions format.	Look at examples of instructions sentences and discuss features and verbs used.
2 Writing and ordering instructions	Sequencing instructions. Discuss an appropriate method of indicating sequence.	Discussing different organisational devices for instructions.	Writing simple instructions sentences and arranging them using simple organisational devices.	Writing simple instructions sentences and arranging them using simple organisational devices.	Looking at children's instructions and discussing style and organisational devices.
3 Paper lanterns	Write instructions in order using link phrases and words.	Following instructions to make a paper lantern.	Using framework of words and phrases to write instructions in sequence.	Using framework of words and phrases to write instructions in sequence.	Looking at link words and phrases. Trying out the instructions.
4 Paper chains	Showing how to make a paper chain. Writing instructions for this.	Revising words for indicating sequential order.	Writing instructions for making a paper chain, using pictures and language of time.	Writing instructions for making a paper chain, using pictures and language of time.	Comparing methods of presenting instructions.
5 Stars	Writing instructions for making a star after watching a demonstration.	Evaluating the instructions.	Presenting instructions for making a star in diagram form only.	Writing instructions for making a star in full sentences.	Comparing diagrammatic and text instructions.

Key assessment opportunities
- Can the children follow instructions and write simple instructions?
- Do they understand the structural features of instructions?
- Do they appreciate the importance of clarity and precision?
- Can they use the language of time to show sequences?
- Can they use diagrams for instructions?

Decorating the tree

Objectives

NLS
T14: To note key structural features, eg sequential steps set out in a list, direct language.
W10: To learn new words from reading linked to particular topics.

What you need
● Photocopiable page 69.

Shared text-level work
● Show the children the diagram and help them to read the labels.
● Explain that they are going to write some instructions for decorating a Christmas tree.
● Write some of the words from the labels in sentences, with the children's help. Emphasise the appropriate register for instructions, which is direct and impersonal and often includes the language of time. Remind the children about their work on 'Hide and seek' and other games.
● Introduce more verbs that could begin instruction sentences for decorating the tree. These could include: *Put, Stand, Hang, Dangle, Drape, Arrange, Place, Fix, Tie, Attach.*
● Establish the meanings of the words, asking children to mime the actions where possible, and write some sentences on the board to illustrate these.

Shared word-level work
● Note some of the unfamiliar words from the labels on photocopiable page 69, such as *baubles, trunk* and *tinsel* and help children to learn to spell them using Look>Say>Cover>Write>Check.
● Look at other words in the labels and relate them to similar familiar words and discuss the common spelling patterns, for example, *star, jar, tar, far* and *lights, night, bright, fight, sight.*

Guided and independent work
● Ask children to write instructions that include the labels on the photocopiable sheet. Remind them that their instructions should be written in complete sentences and ask them to write instructions in the order that they think the actions should take place. Encourage them to write one instruction for each label.
● Help the children to address their instructions directly to the reader by using imperative verbs and keeping their sentences short and simple. Remind them that they can use the displayed list and the example sentences on the board to help them.
● Talk about spellings of words from the labels, write the words down with the children's help and discuss common patterns.

Differentiation

Less able
● Encourage children to work through their instructions orally, but give help with sentence and punctuation.

More able
● Encourage children to think of their own imperative verbs to include in their sentences, and add these to the class word list.

Plenary
● Ask children to share their ideas for sentences. Discuss the verbs they have used and the structure of their sentences.
● Ask children to identify some of the key features of instructional sentences and, with their help, write some more sentences on the board, for example about wrapping presents.
● Look again at some of the words which children have learned during the lesson and discuss their spellings and meanings. Make a display with a labelled Christmas tree so that the children can use this as a word bank. Ask children to brainstorm some Christmas words to add to the word bank.

Writing and ordering instructions

Objectives

NLS
T15: To write simple instructions.
T16: To use models from reading to organise instructions.
S6: To use a variety of simple organisational devices, eg arrows, lines, boxes, to indicate sequences.

What you need
● Photocopiable page 69
● the list of imperative verbs from Hour 1.

Shared text-level work
● Look again at the labelled Christmas tree and work with the children to write instruction sentences on separate pieces of card (or on an interactive whiteboard). Discuss an appropriate order for the sentences and swap the cards around (fixing them with Blu-Tack for instance) until the class is happy with the sequence.
● Ask the children to recall different ways in which the order of steps can be indicated, for example arrows, numbers, boxes in diagrams and experiment with the cards.

Shared sentence-level work
● Reinforce the need for instructions to be easy to read and simple to understand, and remind the children of their work on short, abbreviated sentences or phrases.
● Ask them to give you instructions, in an abbreviated format, for brushing teeth: *Unscrew cap. Pick up toothbrush. Squeeze tube. Put toothpaste on brush. Brush teeth. Rinse mouth. Dry face.* Write each instruction on a separate card, read them through with the children and show them how only key words are included.
● Then ask the children to help you to arrange them in order and to give you ideas for devices that could help to indicate a time sequence, for example numbering, using letters, using time words such as *first, next, then, after that, finally.* Write some time words on cards to show to the children and to use in lesson 3.

Guided and independent work
● Ask children to write their own instructions for an everyday activity such as cleaning teeth, washing hair, writing a letter.
● Encourage them to draw upon the list of imperative verbs produced in the previous lesson where appropriate to write concise instructions.
● Ask them to write each instruction on a separate piece of paper and then to place these on a larger piece and link them using lines and arrows. However, ask the children not to stick their instructions down until you have had chance to discuss the order with them.
● Encourage discussion and sharing of ideas. Talk about different possible sequences for the activities. Ask them which things would need to be done first, which would be best left for last, and which might depend on personal preference.
● Ask children to stick down their sentences, using organisational devices such as arrows and/or lines to show a sequence.

Differentiation

Less able
● Ask children to write instructions for tying their shoelaces.

More able
● Encourage children to produce instructions that require longer sequences and more complex vocabulary.

Plenary
● Ask children to show their instructions to partners and then to the rest of the class. Encourage comments on the sequences used and see if there are alternatives.

Paper lanterns

Objectives

NLS
T11: To use language of time to structure a sequence of events.
T13: To read simple written instructions for constructing something.
W10: To learn new words from reading linked to particular topics.

S&L
14 Listening: To listen to others in class, ask relevant questions and follow instructions.

What you need
● The list of imperative verbs from Hour 1
● teeth-brushing instruction cards from Hour 2
● time words on cards from Hour 2
● coloured paper
● craft materials.

Differentiation

Less able
● Children could draw a picture sequence for making a lantern and then add words from the notes on the board beneath their pictures.

More able
● Ask children to add a handle to their lantern and write additional instructions for this.

Shared text-level work
● Remind the children about the work they have done on using lines and arrows and other devices to link instructions and to indicate the order of steps. Remind them that numbers, bullet points and time words can also be used.
● Display the sequence of cards from the previous lesson. Ask the children for suggestions on how the sequence can be shown by words that link the sentences. For example: _First_ unscrew cap. _Next_ pick up toothbrush. _Then_ squeeze tube. _After that_ put toothpaste on brush. _Now_ brush teeth. _When_ you have finished rinse mouth. _Finally,_ dry face.

Shared word-level work
● Ask the children to watch as you make a paper lantern. Take a piece of coloured paper; fold it; cut about six slits in it, but not right up to the fold; open it out; roll it up and stick the edges together.

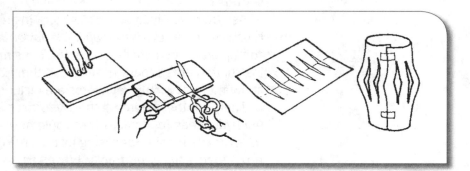

● Make a second lantern and ask the children to tell you what you are doing at each stage. Make notes on the board
● Ask a child to make a lantern following the notes.

Guided and independent work
● Put the time word cards on the board. Ask the children to work in pairs to write sentences that begin with each of the words and phrases, and which form a sequence of instructions for making a paper lantern.
● Children should be able to draw upon the vocabulary presented on the board and the imperative verbs used in Hour 1.
● Discuss time words that could be used to begin their sentences and show the sequence.

Plenary
● Ask children to read out some of their sentences. Choose a sentence to write on the board. Point out the structure and the time words or phrases. Ask the class to suggest a logical preceding and following sentence.
● Either during the plenary or after the lesson, ask children to make lanterns using each other's instructions and then to give feedback to each other on how helpful the instructions are and what could be done to improve them.

Paper chains

Objectives

NLS
T13: To read simple instructions for constructing something.
T17: To use diagrams in instructions, eg drawing and labelling diagrams as part of a set of instructions.
S4: To re-read own writing for sense and punctuation.

S&L
14 Listening: To listen to others in class, ask relevant questions and follow instructions.

What you need
● Strips of coloured paper for making a paper chain.

Shared text-level work
● Show the children, step by step, how to make coloured paper chains to go on a Christmas tree.
● Then ask them to help you to write instructions for making the chains. Write brief sentences at first, for example:

> Cut strips of coloured paper.
> Curl one strip and stick the two ends together to form a ring.
> Pass one end of another strip through the first ring.
> Curl and stick the ends together.
> Continue until you have made a chain.

● Develop these into a clearer sequence by starting each of the first four steps with a time word or phrase. For example, *First, Next, Now, Then.*
● Suggest that the instructions could be presented in a picture sequence and draw a simple picture to show a pair of scissors and strips of paper. Ask the children which written instruction would go with this and write it underneath.

Shared sentence-level work
● Focus on the link words and phrases again and ask children if they can think of any others, for example, *Finally, After that, Secondly, When...* Practise the spelling of any words they suggest.
● Discuss similar words and phrases that would be appropriate for stories but not for instructions, for example *suddenly, once, in the end.* Ask why these don't work in instructions.

Guided and independent work
● Ask children to produce instructions for making a paper chain, using picture sequences with short written instructions.
● Remind children to use words and phrases which link sentences and indicate a sequence.
● Encourage them to look at the instructions produced in shared writing if they need help with spellings, but say that you are especially looking for original sentences with their own ideas and phrasing.
● Emphasise the importance of writing clearly so that handwriting is easy to read and instructions are clear.
● Stop occasionally to discuss children's suggestions and experiment with alternative ways of writing the same instruction.

Plenary
● Look at the children's sequences and discuss whether it would be possible to make a chain using only the pictures or only the text.
● Discuss different ways of phrasing the same instructions and talk about the importance of precision and accuracy.
● Let children make paper chains using each other's instructions and then give feedback on how helpful the instructions are.

Differentiation

Less able
● Encourage children to focus on the diagrams, working in partnership with good writers who can write the text.

More able
● Ask children to include a list of *What you need* and to illustrate items and label them.

Stars

Objectives

NLS
T17: To use diagrams in instructions, eg drawing and labelling diagrams as part of a set of instructions.
S4: To re-read own writing for sense and punctuation.

What you need
● Photocopiable page 69
● thick gold or silver card.

Shared text-level work
● Show the children the Christmas tree diagram again and explain that they are going to write instructions for making one of the decorations.
● Without discussing how you are doing it, make a star for the tree by cutting a piece of gold or silver card into a five- or six-pointed star.
● Now take another piece of card and ask the children to give you an opening instruction for making the star. What do you need to do first?
● Explain that you will be asking someone to make a star by following their instructions, so they will need to be clear and in order. Go through each step, encouraging the children to consider if the instructions jump ahead at any point. For example, do you need to draw the star before cutting it out? At the same time, help the children to understand that they should avoid over complicating the instructions.
● When the children have helped you to write a complete set of instructions, ask someone (classroom assistant or older child perhaps) to follow them to make a star.

Shared sentence-level work
● Examine the finished product. Did the person who made it have to change anything? Talk about the quality of the instructions and about what the features of good, clear instructions are, for example, simple, direct language; sequential steps set out clearly.

Guided and independent work
● Work with a group to produce instructions in diagram form only, drawing upon the sentences produced in shared writing.
● Emphasise the importance of careful presentation and clarity of instructions.
● Remind them to use arrows or lines to show the order of steps.
● Demonstrate how diagrams enable us to be concise and minimise the need for words and phrases. They can be followed quickly and are useful for people who do not read well, or for whom English is not their first language.
● Ask the other children to produce instructions for making a star, using complete sentences.
● Remind them to use time language to indicate the sequence and to write each step on a new line.
● Stop the children occasionally so that they may share their work and comment upon what each other has produced.

Plenary
● Ask children to bring their instructions to the plenary and ask the guided group to show their diagrams to the others.
● Discuss differences between instructions in diagram form and written instructions. Which do they prefer? Which are easier to follow? Can they think of any advantages or disadvantages to one form or the other? Might instructions be suitable in some cases and diagrams in others?

Differentiation

Less able
● Ask children to draft their sequence first to make sure they have included all the steps and in the right order, before drawing or writing a final version.

More able
● Ask children to produce instructions for making a star by drawing two triangles and sticking them together.

Decorated Christmas tree

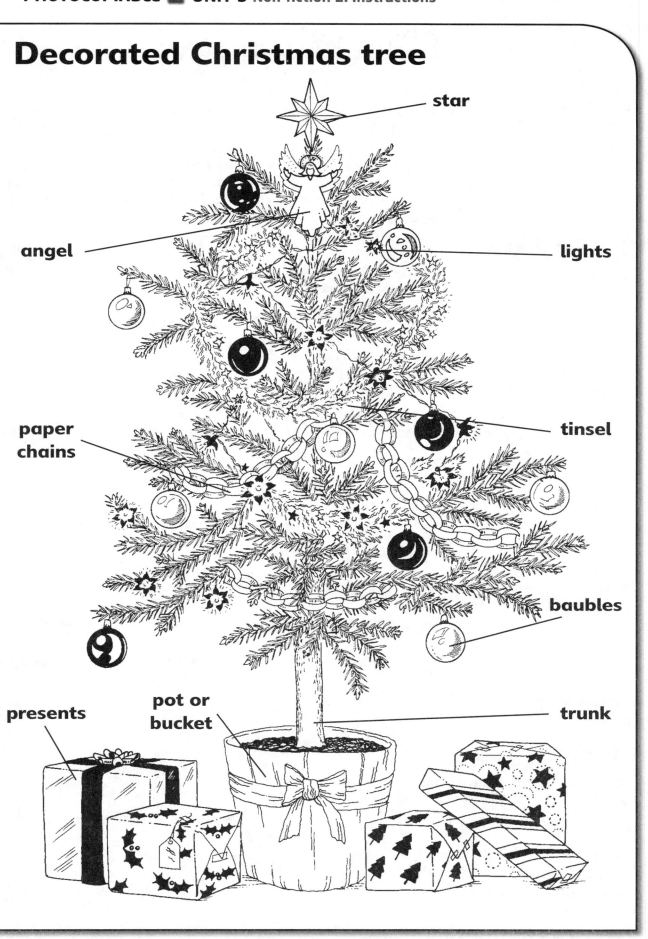

star

angel

lights

paper
chains

tinsel

baubles

presents

pot or
bucket

trunk

UNIT 1 🗨

Narrative 1

This unit is based around a well-known traditional story. It comprises five days' activities supporting the NLS medium-term plan focus on traditional stories. It will help develop children's understanding of setting, character and story structure, as well as developing their knowledge of verb tenses. There will also be opportunities for them to practise reading aloud with expression. This unit also covers *Developing early writing*, units B and E.

Hour	Shared text-level work	Shared word-/ sentence-level work	Guided work	Independent work	Plenary
1 Poor Cinderella 🗨	Reading part 1 of the story. Discussing events and settings	Identifying speech marks and reading dialogue. Role-play.	Writing speech for key characters.	Writing speech and considering performance.	Performing dialogue. Learning alternatives to *said*.
2 Magic	Reading part 2 of the story, focusing on dialogue.	Reading with expression, using dialogue punctuation.	Reading with expression. Writing dialogue.	Practising reading/ reciting with expression.	Performing lines and discussing clues to help the reader to read with expression.
3 Predicting the story	Predicting the story ending.	Identifying verb tenses	Changing present tense to	Changing present tense to past tense in sentences.	Discussing tenses.
4 A happy ending?	Writing of sentences for the story ending.	Thinking of key words. Looking at spelling patterns.	Writing an ending for the story.	Writing an ending for the story.	Sharing story endings and discussing spellings.
5 Describing characters	Discussing characters. Reading part 3 of the story. Comparing endings	Describing characters using lists of adjectives.	Describing characters in longer sentences.	Writing simple sentences that include adjectives separated by commas.	Sharing descriptions of characters. Reinforcing use of commas and sentence punctuation.

Key assessment opportunities
● Can the children identify and understand speech marks?
● Do they use commas to separate items in a list?
● Are they using verb tenses accurately?
● Did they read aloud with expression and intonation?
● Could they predict a story ending and describe characters?

Poor Cinderella

Objectives

Objectives

NLS
T5: To discuss story settings: to compare differences; to locate key words and phrases in text; to consider how different settings influence events and behaviour.
S6: To identify speech marks in reading, understand their purpose, use the terms correctly.

S&L
13 Speaking: To speak with clarity and use intonation when reading and reciting texts.

What you need
● Photocopiable page 76
● envelope containing photocopiable page 79.

Differentiation

Less able
● Help children to make simple notes for dialogue, or use a tape recorder to record their lines.

More able
● Encourage children to write extensively and prepare a performance.

Shared text-level work
● Introduce the story. Ask the children if they have heard the story before and, if so, to tell their partners a little about it.
● Read the first part of the story to the children.
● Explain that this story was written a very long time ago and has been passed down from generation to generation. Many authors have written versions, and films have been made. This means that the versions the children have heard or seen may differ from each other and from this one, but the basic story will still be the same.
● Talk about the events in the story so far and describe the setting (when and where the story takes place).

Shared sentence-level work
● Look at the dialogue and ask three children to read the parts of Cinderella and the stepsisters. Show the children that speech marks surround these words, helping the reader to understand when someone is speaking, while other text tells the reader who is speaking and how their words are said.
● Focus on the arrival of the invitation. Ask another three children to take on the roles of Cinderella and the stepsisters and another to deliver the invitation. Tell the children to act in role as they open the envelope and read the contents. Encourage them to improvise some dialogue, based on what they have been reading.
● Try this again with other children to generate plenty of ideas.
● Then show how the words can be set out in writing. Model the use of speech marks. Ask the children to help you to revise and edit the lines, thinking about how each character would speak.
● Ask children to play Cinderella and her stepsisters and read the new lines.

Guided and independent work
● Support one group in writing dialogue for the receipt of the invitation. Focus on helping them to punctuate speech accurately.
● Ask children to write their own lines of dialogue for the event. They could do this in threes, with each child representing one of the characters. Encourage them to use speech marks.
● Explain that during the plenary you will ask some groups to perform their lines for the class.

Plenary
● Invite groups to perform their dialogue. Encourage them to say the lines with expression. Discuss how this can bring text to life for the listener.
● Write some examples on the board and ask the class to help you to write who spoke and how, for example, shrieked Griselda, shouted Ermintrude, or Cinderella whispered. Remind children to be aware of who is saying what. Would Cinderella or the fairy godmother yell? Would the prince mutter?

Magic

Objectives

NLS

T7: To prepare and retell stories individually and through role-play in groups, using dialogue and narrative from text.
S2: To read aloud with intonation and expression appropriate to the grammar and punctuation (sentences, speech marks, exclamation marks).

What you need
● Photocopiable page 77.

Shared text-level work
● Remind the children about the events in the story from the previous lesson, and explain that in this lesson they will be finding out what happened next.
● Read part 2 to the children. As you read it again with them, ask two children to play the parts of Cinderella and her godmother, reading the words they speak. Remind the children that the speech marks help us to identify speech and separate it from the rest of the text.

Shared word-/sentence-level work
● Pick out at any words that the children don't know or need help to read and talk through them.
● Next, look at the story again and focus on clues that help the reader to read it with the correct expression and tone. You could focus on four examples of speech:

> 'Oh dear,' she said sadly. 'I do wish I could have gone to the palace too.'
> 'But you can!' called a voice from behind her...
> 'Oh, thank you! Thank you!' she cried... 'if only I could get there.'
> 'Let's see about that!' said her godmother.

● Experiment with saying the lines, and ask the children to try saying them to their partners. Talk about the exclamation marks and other punctuation and how they help to indicate how the words are said, for example, loudly, excitedly or quietly, with a sigh. Combine this with the vocabulary used and the message this gives to the reader: *she said sadly* and *she cried*.

Guided and independent work
● Support a group as they read and practise saying the lines spoken by Cinderella and her godmother.
● Encourage them to write additional lines of dialogue within the same scene. Talk about whether exclamation marks would be appropriate and what vocabulary is best to describe how the lines should be said.
● Ask the children to work in pairs to practise the dialogue. Encourage them to learn the lines so that they can perform them for others.
● Tell them that, if they wish, they may write additional lines for the dialogue or change the ones from the shared text.

Plenary
● Ask children to say the lines from the shared text and any others they have written or changed, reading with expression. Discuss the punctuation and vocabulary that is helping them to do so.
● Make a brief comparison of the different versions and remind the children how stories like this often change over time. Research different versions of the story and talk about why it may have changed – perhaps because it has been translated from a different language.

Differentiation

Less able
● Organise children to work with reading partners.

More able
● Ask some of the most able readers to work at each table to read the text aloud when other children encounter problems.

Predicting the story

Objectives

NLS
T4: To predict story endings/incidents, eg from unfinished extracts, while reading with the teacher.
S5: To use verb tenses with increasing accuracy in speaking and writing.
S9: To secure the use of simple sentences in own writing.

What you need

● Photocopiable pages 77 and 80.

Shared text-level work

● Re-read part 2 of the story. Ensure the children have understood it, then ask if they know what happens next. Many of them may already know the story. Let them discuss their predictions in pairs.
● Then ask the children to offer their ideas for the ending and write these on the board in brief sentences or note form. Where children give different or conflicting versions, write each down and link them with *or*. Encourage them to make reference to the text to explain their thoughts.
● Say that they will be able to write their own versions of the story ending in the next lesson.

Shared sentence-level work

● Remind the children that stories tend to be written in the past tense, although speech is usually in the present tense. Pick a sentence from the story that contains dialogue to help explain this.
● Say some sentences that include these verbs in the present tense: *help, clean, brush, button, see, sigh, is, pick*. (They appear in the opening paragraph of part 2, in the past tense.)
● Ask the children to help you to change your sentences from the present to the past tense. For all of the verbs except *is*, this is simply a matter of adding *-ed*. For *is* (the verb *to be*) the past tense is irregular. Say some other parts of this verb in the present tense (*I am, you are, we are, they are*) and ask the children to change them into the past tense. In some areas this may present problems, since the local dialect may, for example, use *was* for all past tense versions of to be (*you was, we was, they was*). However, children do need to understand the Standard English versions, and this may present a good opportunity to talk about these.
● Write some other simple sentences in the present tense that include the verbs above, and work with the children to rewrite them in the past tense.

Guided and independent work

● Ask the children to look at the sentences on photocopiable page 80 and to rewrite them in the past tense. Encourage them to work co-operatively. They may use part 2 of the story to help them to find past tense forms of the verbs.
● Encourage them to write a few more sentences about what they did, for example after school yesterday or last weekend.

Plenary

● Ask the children to share their sentences with classmates.
● Write some of the sentences on the board and discuss the tenses of the verbs.
● Ask the children to make up sentences for each other to change into different tenses. Encourage some to share their sentences with the rest of the class.

Differentiation

Less able
● Ask adults or more able children to help children to read the questions and act as scribes if necessary.

More able
● When they have completed the sentences, ask them to identify verbs in the story and say whether they are past or present.

A happy ending?

Objectives

NLS

T4: To predict story endings/incidents, eg from unfinished extracts, while reading with the teacher.
T12: Through shared and guided writing to apply phonological, graphic knowledge and sight vocabulary to spell words accurately.
W10: To learn new words from reading linked to particular topics.

What you need

● Photocopiable page 77.

Shared text-level work

● Remind the children about the story so far and about the predictions they made about the ending. Re-read part 2 with them.
● Explain that they are going to help you to write the first few sentences of an ending for the story. Talk about some of the story endings they already know and discuss the fact that most of these endings are happy ones.
● Recall the names of the principal characters with the children and ask pairs to discuss what they think might happen to them.
● With the children's help, write an opening sentence for the final part of the story. Talk about the verbs you use and the tense in which they are written. Draw upon the children's ideas to revise and edit the sentence before moving on to the next sentence.
● As you write, occasionally make deliberate mistakes for the children to spot, and ask them to help you to correct them. For example, begin a sentence without a capital letter, miss out a full stop, use the wrong tense of a verb.

Shared word-level work

● To help children to prepare for independent writing, discuss some key story words that they may need. Make a list of these on the board, involving the children in spelling. Ideally, relate the words to others with similar spelling patterns. For example:

> *coach* – talk about other words with *oa* vowel digraph, such as *boat*, *coat*, and *ch* ending, such as *teach*, *reach*.
> *palace* – soft c words, such as *place*, *race*, *lace*
> *Prince* – *-nce* endings, such as *dance*, *mince*, *chance*
> *midnight* – words with *-ight* endings, such as *bright*, *right*, *sight*
> *marry* – look at *carry*, *hurry*, *worry* and so on.

Guided and independent work

● Ask the children to write their own versions of the story ending. If they already know the story they may use this information, or they may decide to change the traditional ending. Advise them to refer to the sentences constructed in shared work.
● Stop the whole class occasionally to share good work.
● Allow time in another literacy lesson or at another time in the day for the children to complete their stories.

Differentiation

Less able
● Ask children to write their story endings in note form or in pictures and words.

More able
● Encourage children to move away from the traditional ending.

Plenary

● Ask children to read their stories to each other and encourage some to read theirs to the whole class.
● Compare any endings where something unusual or unexpected happens with traditional versions.
● Write on the board any words which children have misspelled. Note the correct spellings and relate words to others with similar spelling patterns.

Describing characters

Objectives

NLS
T6: To identify and describe characters, expressing own views and using words and phrases from the text.
S8: To use commas to separate items in a list.

What you need
● Photocopiable page 78.

Shared text-level work
● Recall the story so far and ask the children about the key events.
● Talk about the characters in some detail and ask the children what they think of them so far. Which characters do they like and dislike? Why? (Make sure the children refer to the text.) Can they think of words to describe the different characters?
● Write the names of the key characters on the board and ask the children to suggest adjectives to describe each of them. Write the adjectives as a horizontal list, placing commas between them.
● Read the final part of the story. Help the children with any words they don't understand.
● Ask the children for their thoughts on the story ending. Do they like it? Compare it with their own versions and those in other Cinderella stories they have heard.

Shared sentence-level work
● Look again at the list of characters and the adjectives used to describe them. Using the adjectives for one character, work with the children to write a sentence describing that person, for example, *The Fairy godmother was a very kind lady with a lovely smile* or *Prince Charming was a handsome man with dancing blue eyes.*
● Ask the children to discuss in pairs possible sentences to describe another character. Share some of these and write a few on the board. Model the use of commas and other sentence punctuation.
● Some of the adjectives applied to characters may be antonyms. For example, Cinderella is sad in one part of the story but happy in another. Talk about this and consider different sentences for different parts of the story. For example, *In the first part of the story, Cinderella was... At the end of the story, Cinderella is...*

Guided and independent work
● Ask the children to work in pairs to write at least one sentence to describe each of the following characters: Cinderella, Griselda, Ermintrude, Cinderella's godmother, and the Prince. Remind them to use commas if they use more than one adjective. Begin by brainstorming possible words to use to describe each character, for example, Griselda might be *unkind, boastful, loud.* They may come up with words which are not in the text, but this does not matter as long as they are appropriate to the character.
● Work with a group to support their writing. Talk about the use of commas in lists and help them to write at greater length about the characters.

Differentiation

Less able
● Help the children to punctuate their sentences, but encourage their own ideas for adjectives.

More able
● Encourage pairs to write more than one extended sentence per character, punctuated correctly.

Plenary
● Ask some children to read their sentences to the class. Write these on the board with the children's help.
● Revise correct sentence punctuation and the use of commas in lists and ask the children to suggest further sentences.

Cinderella – part 1

Once upon a time in a faraway kingdom, there lived a girl whose mother had died some years ago. When she was 16, her father married again. This lady, who became the girl's stepmother, had two grown-up daughters of her own. They were very unkind to their new stepsister, and made her do all the work in the house. Because she was now so often covered in ash and soot from the fire, her stepsisters started calling her Cinderella.

One day, a big envelope with a golden crown on it was delivered to the house. When the envelope was opened, the girls found something very exciting. The Prince of the country had decided to get married, but he had not yet chosen his Queen. He was inviting all the young ladies in the land to a ball at the palace, and he would choose one to marry.

The stepsisters were very excited.

"I shall wear my new purple gown," announced Griselda.

"Huh! I shall wear my sparkly orange dress, with my green shoes," said Ermintrude.

"I shall have pink streaks put in my hair," boasted Griselda.

"Really? Well, I shall wear bright blue feathers in mine."

"I shall dance with the Prince at least six times."

"You won't have a chance – he'll be dancing with me all night!"

"We shall have a wonderful time!" said Cinderella.

Her sisters turned round and shrieked, "Cinderella! You have far too many jobs to do! You can't possibly go to the ball!" Poor Cinderella!

Cinderella – part 2

On the night of the ball, Cinderella helped her stepsisters to get ready. She cleaned their shoes and brushed their hair, and buttoned their dresses for them, and saw them off in her father's coach.

Then she sighed, because she was very sad. She picked up the brush ready to carry on sweeping the kitchen floor. "Oh dear," she said sadly. "I do wish I could have gone to the palace too."

"But you can!" called a voice from behind her. Looking round, Cinderella saw a little old lady sitting on a stool in the corner.

"Don't look so alarmed," the woman said gently. "I am your godmother and I have the power of magic. You can go to the palace and dance with the prince, Cinderella."

Cinderella was delighted, but then she remembered – "But I have only this dirty, ragged dress to wear!"

The old lady spoke some magic words and waved her wand, and Cinderella suddenly found herself dressed in a beautiful shining white ball gown. The old sandals she had been wearing had been changed too, into sparkling dancing-shoes of clear glass. They shone like diamonds as she moved her feet.

"Oh, thank you! Thank you!" she cried. "Now I could go to the ball – if only I could get there."

"Let's see about that!" said her godmother. She looked around the

kitchen and found a huge pumpkin. With a wave of her wand, she changed it into a golden coach that Cinderella could ride in. Six mice were turned into fine white horses to pull the coach. "Now you can ride to the palace in your own coach. But you must remember that all my magic can only last until midnight," warned the old lady. "You must be home by midnight, or everything will turn back to the way it was before."

" I'll remember that," promised Cinderella, and with a happy and excited smile, she set off for the palace in her glorious gold coach.

Cinderella – part 3

As soon as Cinderella arrived at the palace, the Prince noticed her. She looked so lovely, smiled so brightly and danced so gracefully. He danced with her all evening and made up his mind that she was the girl he wanted to marry. At last, the music stopped, and the Prince told her, "Since you arrived, I haven't been able to look at another girl in the room. Please, tell me who you are."

Cinderella smiled and was just about to answer when she heard the clock begin to strike. Was it eleven o'clock? No – it was midnight already! Startled, she turned and ran as fast as she could back to the coach. She ran so fast that one of her glass slippers fell off, and she didn't have time to stop to pick it up.

The Prince was very surprised when Cinderella ran away, but he chased after her and was just in time to see her drop her shoe as she jumped into the coach. He picked up the shining slipper and said to himself, "There couldn't be two girls with such tiny and delicate feet. When I find the girl whose foot fits this shoe, I have found my Queen!"

The next morning, Cinderella was back at work as usual in the kitchen when she heard a loud knock at the door. Her two stepsisters peered though the window and, when they saw the Prince waiting, they hurried to answer the knock.

The Prince sounded very tired and sad. "I have been to every house in the city looking for the girl who dropped this shoe last night," he explained. "Yours is the last house, so I am sure she must be here. Please will you try it on?"

The two sisters fought to be the first to try on the tiny glass shoe. They nearly broke it as they tried to force their big feet in, but the Prince could see that it would never fit either of them. "Oh dear," he sighed. "She was a lovely girl, and now I can't find her. Isn't there anyone else in this house who could try the shoe on?"

The sisters shouted, "No!" but, just then, the Prince heard a quiet voice say, "May I try, please?"

He looked further into the room and saw Cinderella, in her old ragged dress, her face and hair dotted with soot and dust. He could hardly see that she was the same beautiful girl he had danced with, but he said, "Yes, of course you may!" and he held out the shoe.

Cinderella slipped her foot into it easily, and when she looked up and smiled, the Prince recognised her. "I have found you!" he cried happily. "Please say that you will marry me!"

"Of course I will," promised a delighted Cinderella.

So Cinderella and the Prince were married and they lived a long, happy life together.

Rosemary Waugh

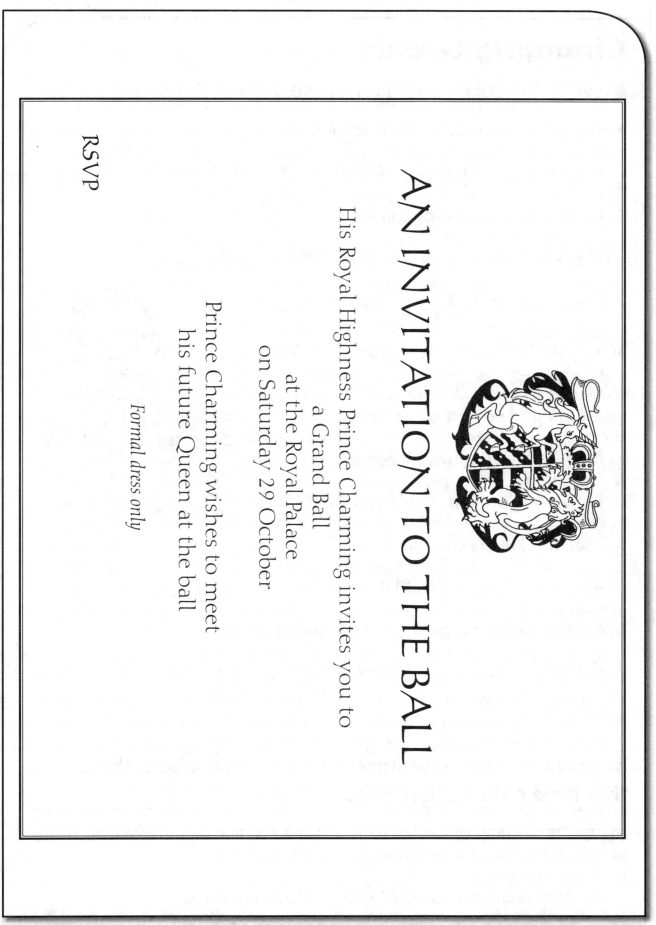

AN INVITATION TO THE BALL

His Royal Highness Prince Charming invites you to

a Grand Ball

at the Royal Palace

on Saturday 29 October

Prince Charming wishes to meet
his future Queen at the ball

Formal dress only

RSVP

TERM 2

Changing tenses

■ Write the correct version of the verb in the space.

1. I help with housework after school.

Last week I _____ with housework after school.

2. I clean my shoes all by myself.

I have always _____ my shoes all by myself.

3. I brush my teeth every morning and

every night.

Last week I _____ my teeth

every morning and every night.

4. I button my coat before I go out.

I _____ my coat before I went out.

5. I see my friend every day.

I _____ my friend yesterday.

6. Cartoons are my favourite television programmes

Cartoons _____ my favourite television programmes when I

was three.

■ Now write some sentences of your own about things
that have already happened.

_____

_____

_____

_____

UNIT 2 📖

Poetry

This unit is based around two poems about cats and supports the medium-term plan focus on work by significant children's poets. The activities will help children to develop their understanding of poetic forms and provide them with opportunities for writing their own verses following the models presented in the poems. The poems should be used to promote discussion and should be read and re-read to enable children to understand the language used by the poets as well as the content. This unit also covers *Progression in phonics*, step 7.

Hour	Shared text-level work	Shared word-/ sentence-level work	Guided work	Independent work	Plenary
1 Cats	Reading poem.	Using context and phonics to decipher unfamiliar words.	Writing own sentences about Danny the cat.	Writing of sentences about Danny to include new words and correct punctuation.	Sharing sentences and practising spellings.
2 Danny the cat	Re-reading the poem and writing a verse about Danny.	Looking at the way in which the poem is presented and the use of repetition.	Writing additional verses for the poem in Zephaniah's style.	Writing additional verses for the poem in Zephaniah's style	Sharing and evaluating verses and comparing with Zephaniah's.
3 Compound words	Reading and discussing another poem	Identifying and brainstorming compound words.	Playing a game to find compound words.	Making compound words.	Sharing examples of compound words to create a class collection.
4 The Farmer's Cat	Writing an additional verse.	Learning spellings of unfamiliar words form the poem.	Re-reading the poem before writing an additional verse.	Writing an additional verse and prepare for reading aloud.	Sharing new verses. Practising spellings.
5 Poems about cats	Building up a poem about cats.	Looking at verb tenses and adjectives.	Writing simple, structured lines for a poem.	Writing simple, structured lines for a poem.	Sharing lines and creating a class poem. Setting up cat poetry display.

Key assessment opportunities
● Do the children use grammar and context to help with unfamiliar words?
● Can they split compound words?
● Can they identify structures in simple poems?
● Can they write their own verses?

Cats

Objectives
T2: To use phonological, contextual, grammatical and graphic knowledge to work out, predict and check the meanings of unfamiliar words and to make sense of what they read.
S1: To use awareness of grammar to decipher new or unfamiliar words.
W10: To learn new words from reading linked to particular topics.

What you need
● Photocopiable page 87.

Shared text- and sentence-level work
● Read the poem to the children and then read it with them, enjoying the images created.
● Talk about the poem's repetitive nature, and how this structure suits the cat subject. Ask children who have cats to compare their cats' behaviour with that described in the poem. Do they think that Danny the cat has a nice life? How does it compare with what they and their families do every day? What are the similarities and differences?
● Re-read the poem, pausing at unfamiliar words. Demonstrate how to use context to work out what the words might mean. For example, Danny… finds a cosy place and sleeps. Children might attempt to work out the word cosy by sounding c (as cat) o (as cot) and so on, but if they consider the context too and the fact that Danny goes to sleep, they may be able to determine that the word is cosy, which they probably have heard but may not have seen.

Shared word-level work
● List some of the unfamiliar words and phrases on the board and work through their sounds and meanings. These might include: *private, inspects, cosy, climbs, claws, nature, programme, stroked.*
● Read the words within the text and ask children to use context and grammatical structure to help them to work out what the words mean. Suggest that they use dictionaries to confirm meanings.
● Talk about words that have similar sound patterns to some of those discussed, for example *rosy, nosey, dozy; combs, thumb, limb, dumb; draw, gnaw, thaw.* Note the spellings and practise the sounds made by individual letters, blends and digraphs.

Guided and independent work
● Ensure that the group can see the list of unfamiliar words on the board, and then support them as they use the words in their own sentences about cats. Discuss spellings and sentence structure with them as they work.
● Ask children to work in pairs to write their sentences about cats. Remind them that sentences should begin with capital letters and end with full stops, exclamation marks or question marks. Quickly revise other correct usage of these.
● Ask them to read their sentences to each other to check that they are complete. Encourage them to work together on revisions. Remind them not only to check for spelling, punctuation and grammar, but to look at vocabulary and style.

Plenary
● Share the children's sentences. Ask some children to read their sentences aloud. Write these on the board, seeking the rest of the children's help with spellings.
● Quickly point to some of the words in the list and ask the children to read them with you.

Differentiation

Less able
● Provide partially completed sentences to be filled in with words from the board.

More able
● Ask children to write more complex sentences.

Danny the cat

Objectives

NLS

T15: To use structures from poems as a basis for writing, by extending or substituting elements, inventing own lines, verses.

S7: To investigate and recognise a range of ways of presenting texts.

What you need

● Photocopiable page 87
● a selection of notices for the classroom
● props for a 'playing schools' role-play area including a teacher's chair and easel
● high frequency words on card.

Shared text- and sentence-level work

● Re-read the poem with the children. Show how the lines in bold work as subheadings for the things Danny gets up to. Notice how many times Danny wakes up – implying that he sleeps an awful lot! Ask too what Danny does most often on waking. (Eats.)

● Ask the children to help you to write an additional verse in the same style. Begin the verse with Danny wakes up, and draw upon the children's ideas and their sentences from the previous lesson for ideas.

● Make notes on the board of the children's suggestions, before writing the verse. Talk about the importance of thinking ideas through before beginning to write. As you and the children choose an idea for each line, look at Zephaniah's poem to help you construct the line. For example, use few words, begin with a verb and so on.

● When the short verse has been completed, ending with *And sleeps*, read it aloud with the children and then ask them if they would like to change it any way. Compare the verse with some of Zephaniah's and see if it follows a similar pattern.

● As well as noting the use of bold type, talk more about the layout of the poem, and the use of capital letters to begin each line.

● Discuss the use of repetition of style in the poem and draw the children's attention to examples of this. For example, the lines *And sleeps* and *Danny wakes up* are repeated regularly and used to indicate the end of one section and the beginning of another.

Guided and independent work

● Ask the children to draw upon the sentences they wrote in Hour 1 and to look at the poem again to write further verses in pairs. Remind them that their verse should tell further adventures of Danny. Tell them to talk through their ideas and make notes before they begin more structured writing.

● Encourage the children to check that they are following a similar pattern to that Zephaniah has used and are presenting their verse(s) in the same style.

● Guide a lower ability group to support the children's writing and to discuss the structure of the poem.

Plenary

● Bring the children together and ask some to read the verses they have produced. Write some of these on the board and praise the authors.

● Address any spelling and style errors and ask for contributions about ways in which children could improve their verses. Encourage these ideas to be positive and to include general points useful for all poetry writing.

● Compare the children's verses with Benjamin Zephaniah's. Ask if the new ones make suitable additions and encourage the children to justify their thoughts.

Differentiation

Less able
● Encourage independent ideas, but model the writing if necessary.

More able
● Ask children to write more than one verse and to make use of dictionaries and thesauruses.

Compound words

Objectives

NLS
T9: To identify and discuss patterns of rhythm, rhyme and other features of sound in different poems.
W4: To split familiar oral and written compound words into their component parts.
W10: To learn new words from reading linked to particular topics.

What you need
● Photocopiable pages 87–89
● coloured paper or card.

Shared text-level work
● Read 'The Farmer's Cat' to the children and then with them.
● Talk about what the cat does, and compare these with the things Danny did in the previous poem. Notice that this poem also uses a repetitive structure.
● Ask the children if they can explain the final two verses in which the cat plants tiny fish and dreams of harvesting fish in the autumn. Do they think this would be possible? Why does the cat think it would? Look back at earlier verses and discuss what the cat has followed the farmer doing.

Shared word-level work
● Write the word indoors on the board and ask the children if they remember it from the poem about Danny. Demonstrate that it is a compound word made up of two words – in and doors. Together, find compound words in 'The Farmer's Cat': *raindrops*, *peanuts*, and even the poet's surname, Greygoose.
● Ask the children if they can think of further compound words. Help them by writing some words which could form part of compound words, for example, *hair* (hairbrush), *tooth* (toothbrush), *foot* (football, footwear), *some* (someone, somebody, something).
● Show how we can often break longer words into parts to help us to read them. Develop this into a long list of compound words. You may need to suggest some to keep up the momentum, for example *daytime*, *playtime*, *classroom*, *bookmark*, *handbag*.

Guided and independent work
● Give the children the word cards from photocopiable page 88 so that they can try making pairs to make compounds. Spread out the cards face down and ask the children to take turns to choose a pair and decide if the two words could be formed into one word. When they have formed a word, ask them to write it down and then turn the cards over again for the next person's turn.
● Ask the children to see how many words they can make from those on photocopiable page 88.
● Encourage them to create further compound words by adding words not in the list to those that are.

Differentiation

Less able
● Provide compound words for children to identify the two words that form them.

More able
● Ask children to look for compound words in their reading books and to identify the words that form them.

Plenary
● See how many compound words the children have made. Did they manage to use every card?
● Write some on the board and ask the children to check for you by identifying the two words that have been put together.
● Begin a class collection of compound words by asking children to write three of the words they made on individual pieces of coloured paper. Display the words in alphabetical order. Ask children to make up their own compound words and define them, reminding them that these are not real words to be used in their writing.

The Farmer's Cat

Objectives

NLS
T8: To read own poems aloud.
T15: To use structures from poems as a basis for writing, by extending or substituting elements, inventing own lines, verses.
W10: To learn new words from reading linked to particular topics.

What you need
● Photocopiable page 88.

Shared text- and word-level work
● Re-read the poem. Focus on style and structural points, such as the refrains, the repetitive events and language, the short verse followed by a longer verse.
● With the children's help, write further verses about what the cat might have seen and made her think that she could grow a fish crop in the fields.
● Make a list of crops that could be grown, including wheat and beetroot. Go through the spelling of each word.
● Follow the pattern of 'The Farmer's Cat' carefully. This means that in the first new verse only the fourth line will change, and in the second verse only the fifth line will change. To emphasise this, write on the board the lines that will remain constant and then write children's ideas as final lines for each part of the verse.
● Now read the verse with the children. Make any necessary improvements and re-read it together.
● As you write any additional verses, help the children to learn the spellings of the words they suggest.

Guided and independent work
● Support one of the groups as they re-read 'The Farmer's Cat'. Discuss the poem in detail with the children in terms of its structure and vocabulary.
● Help them to write additional verses describing something else the cat sees the farmer planting and growing. Refer to the verses you wrote together and the word list of crops. Tell the children to use their imaginations to think of more crops that the farmer could grow.
● Stop the group occasionally to hear them read their work and address any problems with spelling. Make sure that they are using dictionaries to check their spellings.
● Ask the children to work individually or in pairs to produce additional verses for 'The Farmer's Cat'.
● When they have written their verses ask them to practise reading them aloud with expression in preparation for performing them in the plenary. Ask more able children to think about the particular characteristics of a cat. How might the farmer's dog or horse behave? Ask children to start a poem about another farm animal.

Differentiation

Less able
● Provide a cloze-type writing frame to complete using words from the board.
● Pair the children with more able partners.

More able
● Children could go on to write further verses and use reference books to find other crops to include.

Plenary
● Share the new verses. Ask some children to read theirs aloud. Encourage them to do so with appropriate expression and intonation. Talk again about how this helps the listener to understand and enjoy the poem.
● Read the whole poem, with one of the children's verses in place, and consider how well it fits.
● Write on the board some of the new words the children have used. Ask the children to learn the spellings using Look>Say>Cover>Write>Check and, if appropriate, let them test each other.

Poems about cats

Shared text-level work

● Recall the two poems about cats and re-read them.
● Ask the children to tell you about any cats or kittens they know – either their own cats or cats from books, cartoons, films and so on.
● As you name some types of cat ask the children for help in spelling them. Begin a list that could include grey, tabby, black, white, striped, ginger.
● Ask the children how to describe the nature or behaviour of cats, for example *speedy, sleepy, slinky, sneaky, quiet*. Add these to the words on the board: *Slinky black cat, Sleepy striped cat.*
● When you have two adjectives for each line, ask the children to read the list with you quite quickly. Explain that you have written a kind of poem.
● Now ask the children if they can make the poem more interesting by adding a verb to each line, describing what cats get up to, for example *Slinky black cat jumping, Sleepy striped cat snoozing.*

Shared sentence-level work

● Talk about the tense which is used for the verbs in the poem (present). Help them to identify this by the -ing ending, and show how it has been used consistently in the poem.
● When the poem has been completed, ask the children if they can tell you how to change the verbs if we were to rewrite the poem in the past tense, for example Slinky black cat jumped, Sleepy striped cat snoozed.
● Add to the list of adjectives and adverbs the children might like to use in their own poems, for example, *quick, soft, furry, fierce, friendly, careful, sly, playful.*

Guided and independent work

● Ask the children to write simple adjective–noun or adjective–noun–verb lines for a poem about cats, continuing that started in shared work. Emphasise that the basic structure is a list and that the lines to do not need to rhyme (although don't discourage children from this). Encourage them to jot down ideas or even make sketches before writing out lines.
● Some children may be able to include verbs and even adverbs. If appropriate, use the opportunity to talk about parts of speech and the jobs they do.

Plenary

● Share the children's poems. Write examples of interesting lines on the board and choose some together to create a class poem. Demonstrate how, as they have all been working to the same structure, lines should be fairly interchangeable.
● Pick out any alliteration or rhyme and talk about different ways in which poems are presented.
● Create a display of cat poetry based around the children's work. Display the poems on silhouette shapes of cats in various poses.

A Day in the Life of Danny the Cat

Danny wakes up
Eats
Finds a private place in the garden,
He returns
Plays with the plants
And sleeps.

Danny wakes up
Eats
Inspects the garden
Finds a cosy place
And sleeps.

Danny wakes up
Comes indoors
Inspects the carpet
Scratches himself
And sleeps

Danny wakes up
Goes into the garden
Over the fence
Has a fight with Ginger
Makes a date with Sandy
Climbs on to next door's shed
And sleeps.

Danny wakes up
Comes indoors
Rubs up the chair leg
Rubs up a human leg
Sharpens his claws
On a human leg
Eats
And sleeps.

Danny wakes up
Eats
Watches a nature programme
Finds a private place in the garden,
Finds Sandy in next door's garden
Next door's dog finds Danny
Sandy runs north

Danny runs home
Eats and sleeps.

Danny wakes up
Checks for mice
Checks for birds
Checks for dogs
Checks for food
Finds a private place in the garden
Eats
And sleeps.

Danny has hobbies,
Being stroked
Car-watching
And smelling feet
He loves life,
Keeps fit
And keeps clean,
Every night he covers himself
In spit,
Then he eats
And sleeps.

Benjamin Zephaniah

The Farmer's Cat

(after a translation from the Chinese
by Xia Liu)

Out in the fields
in spring time,
the farmer's cat follows him
as he plants the seeds of corn.

The cat dances with the raindrops
and sleeps in the sun
and when the autumn comes
she sees that the farmer
has a field full of corn.

Out in the fields
in spring time,
the farmer's cat follows him
as he plants the peanut seeds.

The cat dances with the raindrops
and sleeps in the sun
and when the autumn comes
she sees that the farmer
has a field full of tasty peanuts..

Out in the fields
in spring time,
the farmer watches while his cat
plants rows of tiny fish.

The cat dances with the raindrops
and sleeps in the sun
and dreams that when autumn
comes
she will fill her dish
with all the silver fish
that she's grown in the farmer's
fields.

David Greygoose

Making compound words

◾ How many compound words can you make using these words? Use each word as often as you like.

brush	hand	tooth	hair
bag	basin	water	time
shoe	head	teacher	fall
ache	case	book	play
mark	toe	screw	nail
driver	box	paint	snow
tool	story	door	knob

handbag

UNIT 3

Categorising alphabetically

This unit is based around statistics and other information on popular children's names and comprises literacy activities that focus on alphabetically ordered texts. This should help children to develop the skills needed when using reference sources such as dictionaries, indexes and glossaries. It will also develop children's understanding of tables and charts and recognition of syllables. The children will also be improving their ability to write simple sentences. The activities link to work in other subject areas such as mathematics (reading, presenting and analysing data). This unit also covers *Progression in phonics*, step 5 and step 7.

Hour	Shared text-level work	Shared word-/sentence-level work	Guided work	Independent work	Plenary
1 Popular first names	Reading lists of popular names.	Discussing pronunciation of names, focusing on consonant digraphs *th* and *ch*.	Identifying consonant digraphs and finding words with similar sounds.	Identifying consonant digraphs and finding words with similar sounds.	Discussing collections of *ch* words.
2 Alphabetical order	Arranging names in alphabetical order.	Sounding worcs by breaking them into parts.	Making a combined alphabetical list of boys' and girls' names.	Placing name cards in alphabetical order.	Reinforcing alphabetical order using names in the class.
3 Meanings of names	Reading a glossary chart of meanings of names.	Writing simple sentences to answer questions.	Using the glossary to write answers to questions.	Using the glossary to write answers to questions	Discussing sentence structures.
4 Syllables	Reading meanings of the children's names.	Clapping syllables in names. Identifying names by the number of syllables.	Sorting by syllables and alphabetical order. Looking at other proper nouns.	Sorting names according to syllables and using alphabetical order.	Playing a game of quickfire syllable counting.
5 Popular names in the past	Comparing modern names with those from earlier generations, using ordinal numbers.	Writing simple sentences about the information in the charts.	Answering questions in complete sentences.	Answering questions in complete sentences.	Reviewing work on sentences, syllables and alphabetical order.

Key assessment opportunities
- Can the children distinguish different *ch* sounds?
- Can they put short lists of words into alphabetical order?
- Can they discriminate syllables?
- Did they write sentences?

Popular first names

Objectives

NLS
T16: To use dictionaries to locate words by using initial letters.
W3: To read and spell words containing the digraph *ch*.

What you need
● Photocopiable page 96.

Shared text-level work
● Display the chart of popular names, and explain that it shows which names are given to the most children in the UK.
● Read through the list of boys' names. Note any class members on the list and ask the children if they know anyone else with the names.
● Explain that the popularity of certain boys' names has changed over time. The name John, for example, was given to almost half of all boys at periods in the middle ages because the local lord named children rather than their parents, and often called the boys after themselves. In many families more than one child could be called John! Although John no longer features in the list of most popular names, Jack is top of the list and is a traditional familiar name for boys called John.
● Now read through the girls' names, again discussing them and noting any children who have the same names.

Shared word-level work
● Remind the children that names begin with capital letters.
● Talk about the pronunciation and spelling of some of the names. Focus on Chloe, Charlie and Charlotte, which have the consonant digraph *ch*, but are pronounced in different ways.
● Write the names across the top of the board and ask the children to tell you other 'ch' words they know. Help them to decide which pronunciation column to put them in, for example:

Chloe	Charlie	Charlotte
Christ Christopher school	chips chocolate cheese	chef parachute

● You will almost certainly find that the children are able to think of lots of words to list under Charlie, fewer to list under Chloe, and very few to list under Charlotte.
● Look next at Thomas and Ethan and explain that sometimes th is pronounced *t* as in *toy* but usually is pronounced *th* as in *this*. There are very few examples of *th* sounded as in Thomas, but you may wish to draw attention to the slight difference in pronunciation between words like *this, that, the, them, then*, and *think, throw, through, theme*.

Guided and independent work
● Organise the children to work in pairs to use dictionaries to find words that begin with *ch* and ask them to sort these according to their pronunciation, under the headings Chloe, Charlie and Charlotte.

Plenary
● Ask the children to share their lists.
● Add some of their words to the class list and practise the different ways in which *ch* can be sounded.
●Encourage the children to find more 'ch' words at home for adding to the class list.

Differentiation

Less able
● Guide children's use of dictionaries and practise alphabetical order.

More able
● Using dictionaries that include pronunciation guidance, children could go on to classify words beginning with th under the headings Thomas, think and that.

Alphabetical order

Objectives

NLS
T18: To use alphabetically ordered texts.
W5: To discriminate, orally, syllables in multi-syllabic words using children's names.

What you need
● Photocopiable page 96
● cards from photocopiable page 97
● a large alphabet displayed near the board.

Shared text-level work
● Show the children the chart again and ask them to explain why the names are listed in their present order. (In order of most popular.)
● Ask the children why alphabetical order is useful when we need to find information. (It helps us to know where to look in a document or book – if a word begins with A it will be near the beginning of the book or document and so on.)
● Begin by looking at the first two girls' names: Chloe and Ellie. Attach the name cards to the board. Say the alphabet with the children, pointing to the letters. Then ask which of the two names should come first in an alphabetical list. Put the cards in order.
● Next look at the first two boys' names: Jack and Joshua. Ask how to decide which name comes first alphabetically when both have the same first letter. Talk about using the second letter to arrange the names.
● Show the Emily card and ask the children where to place it in the list of girls' names. Add Thomas and then James and Daniel to the boys' list.
● You will need to explain that where the second letters are the same we look at the third letters and so on, for example in Ellie and Ella, Emma and Emily.

Shared word-level work
● Identify names that children have found difficult to read and show them how to break the word into parts. For example, Sophie and Joseph each have an f sound made by ph; *William, Callum, Ellie, Ella, Molly* and *Holly* all have double l, showing us where to place the stress, while Emily has a single l and three syllables so there is less stress placed on the *l* part.

Guided and independent work
● Work with a group to support them as they arrange the girls' name cards into alphabetical order.
● When they have finished, give them, one at a time, boys' names to insert into their lists, so that they have a combined list of alphabetised boys' and girls' names. Remind the children to look at the second, and, if necessary, third and fourth letters when placing words that begin with the same letter.
● Provide pairs of children with sets of either boys' or girls' names and ask them to arrange them in alphabetical order on their tables.

Differentiation

Less able
● Provide fewer name cards and ask a pair of more able pupils to give support.

More able
● Children could go on to add names of other children in the class.

Plenary
● Write on cards the names of children in the class whose names do not feature in the lists. Ask the children in question to help you to spell their names. Then ask the class to help you to sort them into alphabetical order.
● Tell the children that in the next lesson they will be looking at meanings of names. Ask them to find out why their parents chose their names, but be sensitive to family situations.

Meanings of names

Objectives

NLS
T17: To learn that dictionaries and glossaries give definitions and explanations.
T20: To make class dictionaries and glossaries of special interest words, giving definitions.
S9: To secure the use of simple sentences in own writing.

What you need
● Photocopiable pages 96 and 98
● a book on names and their meanings and/or access to a website.

Shared text-level work
● Explain that one function of first names is to help us distinguish people with the same surname. Our parents choose first names for many reasons. It may be that we are named after a relative or a famous person, or they may simply like the sound of the name or even make up the name. Some people choose names because of what they mean. Ask if they found out why their parents chose their names.
● Show the children the meanings of popular names and help them to locate any names of members of the class.
● Read some of the meanings. (These have been simplified and some books and websites provide detailed information.) Several of the names have biblical derivations. Most of these are pre-Christian and exist in Jewish families too.
● Explain the layout of the table, showing the children how to look at the columns and then scan down the list to find the name they want before looking across to find its meaning. Ask a few questions to establish understanding. For example:

> Which name means 'rich'?
> Which name means 'hard-working'?
> What does the name Chloe mean?

Shared sentence-level work
● With the children's help, write some simple sentences to answer the questions you are asking. Explain that it is important to answer in full sentences so that anyone reading the answers (without the questions) would be able to understand them. For example, if they simply wrote Jessica for the first question above, no one would know what they were referring to, but if they wrote something like, The name Jessica means 'rich', this would be easy to understand.

Guided and independent work
● Give copies of photocopiable pages 96 and 98 to pairs of children and ask them to use the table to answer the questions. Encourage them to discuss their answers and take turns to write them down. Remind them to write full sentences.
● Stop occasionally to discuss some of the meanings that may be hard to understand, for example Chloe and Lauren.
● Help the children to look up their own names in books and on websites. Aim to use at least two sources, as definitions vary.

Differentiation

Less able
● Help children to sound and read the names as many are phonetically irregular.

More able
● Ask children to write their own sentences about other names. Given the lack of names from some ethnic groups in the lists, this is an opportunity to introduce names common in other cultures.

Plenary
● Share the children's answers to photocopiable page 98.
● Talk about sentence structure and praise examples of interesting and accurate phrasing. Compare any different ways in which children have presented their sentences.
● If the children using books/websites have found other common names, discuss some of these too.

UNIT 3 HOUR 4 Categorising alphabetically

Syllables

Objectives

NLS
T18: To use alphabetically ordered texts.
W5: To discriminate, orally, syllables in multi-syllabic words using children's names.

What you need

● Photocopiable page 96
● meanings for names of some children who did not feature in the most popular list, written on large pieces of paper
● name cards for each child in the class (a set for each pair).

Shared text-level work

● Give the children their name meanings before the lesson.
● Ask those children to come to the front. Help them to read their 'definitions' to the class, then attach them to the board.
●Compare the meanings with those in the previous lesson.

Shared word-level work

● Ask three children with different numbers of syllables in their names to come to the front. Show the children how to clap the syllables so that, for example, Jack would have one clap, Sophie would have two, and Natalie would have three.
● Ask children to take turns to clap one of the three names and ask the rest of the class to identify the name.
● Go on to clap the names of other children in the class and ask the children to raise their hands if their name has the same number of syllables.
● Show the list of most popular names and ask the children to identify boys' names with one syllable (Jack, James, Ben, and Luke). Do the same for girls (Grace).
● Next find boys' names with two syllables. Ask the children to do this in pairs by tapping their fingers on the palms of their hands to silently 'clap' the syllables, and to check with each other.
● Go on to look at the girls' names in the sane way, before looking for three-syllable names.
● Only one name has four syllables – Olivia. Ask the children if they can find the four-syllable name.

Guided and independent work

● Give out the sets of name cards and ask the children to work in small groups to sort them first according to the number of syllables each has.
● Once they have done this, ask them to sort each syllable set into alphabetical order and then write the lists in a chart. For example:

1 syllable	2 syllables	3 syllables	4 syllables
Anne	Demi	Emily	Olivia
Ben	Richard	Muhammed	Elizabeth
Luke	Safraz	Christopher	Victoria

● Work with a higher ability guided group, discussing syllables and going on to look at other names such as surnames, place names and book titles.

Plenary

● Discuss the children's classification of the names and address any misconceptions about syllables and alphabetical order. Share dictionaries and indexes to emphasise what they have learned.
● Have a quickfire game of syllable counting. Say a name and see how quickly the children can say (or write on whiteboards) how many syllables it has. Or, for a greater challenge, ask them to come up with another name with the same number of syllables.

Differentiation

Less able
● Prepare files for children to use a computer to create a table for their lists, cutting and pasting to move and sort names.

More able
● See Guided and independent work.

Popular names in the past

Objectives

NLS

T18: To use alphabetically ordered texts.

S4: To be aware of the need for grammatical agreement in speech and writing, matching verbs to nouns/pronouns correctly.

S5: To use verb tenses with increasing accuracy in speaking and writing.

What you need

● Photocopiable pages 99 and 100.

Shared text-level work

●Use this lesson to revisit some of the objectives from previous lessons including sentences, alphabetical order and syllables.

● Show the children the top of photocopiable page 99 and read the lists of names.

● Help the children to understand how the table is organised in terms of row and column headings.

● Write the numbers 1 to 10 down the left-hand side of the board, then write *st* next to 1. Talk about coming first in a race and so on. Next to this, write the word first. Go on to write 2nd, 3rd... and the words, second, third... Use them to ask questions about the table, such as *What is the third name in the list?*

● Identify names that have been popular for many years (appearing several times in the table) and others that are no longer popular.

● Write some incomplete sentences and ask the children to add the missing words. For example:

> ___ was the most popular girls' name in 1994.
> Edith was the ___ most popular name in 1904.
> The first name on the list of girls' names for 2003 is ___.

Shared sentence-level work

● Write sentences to compare popular names of the past with those of the present. For example, George and Arthur were popular names in 1904 but were not in the top five in 1934, 1964, 1994 or 2003. Thomas was a popular name in 1904 and became popular again in 1994 and 2003.

● Note the structure of the sentences. Look at the verb *to be*, which is used in the past tense (*was, were*) when we write about names that used to be popular, but in the present tense when we write about names that are currently popular.

● Emphasise the importance of capital letters for names as well as for the beginnings of sentences.

Guided and independent work

● Provide individuals with both photocopiable sheets and ask them to answer the questions in complete sentences. Recap how to read down and across in the table, depending on the question.

● Stop the children occasionally to look at the questions and assess understanding of alphabetical order and syllables.

Differentiation

Less able

● Prepare cloze sentences or sentence starters for the answers.

More able

● Using the bottom of photocopiable page 99, ask children to write sentences comparing these with the meanings of names from 2003.

Plenary

● Assess children's understanding of syllables and alphabetical order, and their skill at writing complete sentences.

● Look at some of the children's sentences, drawing attention to good work and using the opportunity to address any misconceptions.

● Ask the children what they found interesting about their investigations into names.

TERM 2

Meanings of the most popular names in 2003

Poll commissioned by Bounty based on names of 150,000 babies born in 2003, www.bounty.com

	Boys	Meaning		Girls	Meaning
1	Jack	God has shown favour	1	Chloe	Blooming
2	Joshua	Lord is gracious	2	Ellie	Light
3	Thomas	A twin	3	Emily	Hard-working
4	James	Replace	4	Jessica	Rich
5	Daniel	God is my judge	5	Sophie	Wisdom
6	Lewis	Famous in battle	6	Megan	A pearl
7	Oliver	The olive tree	7	Lucy	Light
8	Matthew	Gift of God	8	Katie	Pure
9	Harry	Army leader	9	Olivia	Olive
10	Ben	Short for Benjamin	10	Charlotte	Little, feminine
11	William	Protector	11	Hannah	Grace of God
12	Ethan	Strong	12	Amy	Beloved
13	Joseph	God will increase	13	Holly	Holy
14	Luke	Light	14	Emma	Complete
15	Adam	The first man	15	Lauren	Laurel-crowned
16	Samuel	Name of God	16	Ella	Light
17	Callum	A dove	17	Mia	Mine
18	Ryan	Little king	18	Grace	Grace of God
19	Benjamin	Son	19	Molly	The perfect one
20	Charlie	Manly	20	Caitlin	Pure

◣ SCHOLASTIC

Name cards

Jack	Joshua	Thomas	James
Daniel	Lewis	Oliver	Matthew
Harry	Ben	William	Ethan
Joseph	Luke	Adam	Samuel
Callum	Ryan	Benjamin	Charlie

Chloe	Ellie	Emily	Jessica
Sophie	Megan	Lucy	Katie
Olivia	Charlotte	Hannah	Amy
Holly	Emma	Lauren	Ella
Mia	Grace	Molly	Caitlin

About the names

1. What does the name Lewis mean?

_____

2. What does the name Kate mean?

_____

3. Which name is short for Benjamin?

_____

4. Which four names all mean 'light'?

_____

5. Which name means 'the first man'?

_____

6. Which girl's names mean 'grace of God'?

_____

7. Which girl's name means 'the perfect one'?

_____

Popular names from 1904 to 2003

		1904	1934	1964	1994	2003
Boys	1st	William	John	David	Thomas	Jack
	2nd	John	Peter	Paul	James	Joshua
	3rd	George	William	Andrew	Jack	Thomas
	4th	Thomas	Brian	Mark	Daniel	James
	5th	Arthur	David	John	Matthew	Daniel
Girls	1st	Mary	Margaret	Susan	Rebecca	Chloe
	2nd	Florence	Jean	Julie	Lauren	Ellie
	3rd	Doris	Mary	Karen	Jessica	Emily
	4th	Edith	Joan	Jacqueline	Charlotte	Jessica
	5th	Dorothy	Patricia	Deborah	Hannah	Sophie

Source: National Statistics website: www.statistics.gov.uk. Crown copyright material is reproduced with the permission of the Controller of HMSO

Meanings of some names popular before 2003

Boys	Meaning	Girls	Meaning
George	tiller of the soil	Florence	flowering
Arthur	follower of Thor	Doris	sharp
Brian	strong one	Edith	rich war
David	friend or beloved	Dorothy	gift of God
Andrew	brave	Margaret	pearl
Mark	warlike	Jean	merciful
		Mary	the perfect one
		Joan	god is gracious
		Patricia	noble
		Susan	lily
		Julie	youthful
		Karen	pure
		Jacqueline	to protect
		Deborah	to speak kind words
		Rebecca	to tie

Popular names in the last 100 years

◼ Look at the table and answer the questions.

1. _____ was the most popular boy's name in 1904.

2. _____ was the most popular boy's name in 1934.

3. _____ was the most popular girl's name in 1904.

4. _____ was the most popular girl's name in 1964.

5. What was the most popular girl's name in 1934?

6. Which names were popular in both 1994 and 2003?

7. Which boys' names have been popular in three of the years?

8. Put the most popular boys' names in each year in alphabetical order.

9. Put the most popular girls' names in each year in alphabetical order.

10. List the boys' names in the table which have 2 syllables.

11. List the girls' names in the table which have 3 syllables.

12. Which boy's name and which girl's name in the lists do you like best?

UNIT 4

Narrative 2

This unit is based around three traditional stories from different cultures. It will help develop children's appreciation of story structure, theme and setting, and enable them to explore characters and the features typical of traditional tales. In addition, there is work on extending vocabulary and on writing simple sentences, as well as on using syntax and semantics to aid reading and understanding of unfamiliar words.

Hour	Shared text-level work	Shared word-/ sentence-level work	Guided work	Independent work	Plenary
1 Story themes	Reading and discussing part 1 of 'The Thick Fat Pancake'.	Focusing on speech marks.	Working out unfamiliar words.	Practising reading in role.	Performing dialogue. Revising speech marks.
2 Predicting the ending	Speculating on and writing what will happen next. Focusing on syllables and sentence construction.	Breaking down multi-syllabic words.	Independent writing of final part of story.	Independent writing of final part of story.	Sharing and comparing the children's versions.
3 Comparing the endings	Reading the second half of the story and relating its theme to other stories.	Looking at words that have the same sounds represented by different letters.	Changing present tense sentences into past tense. Finding past-tense verbs in other books.	Changing present tense sentences into past tense.	Changing more sentence, focusing on irregular spellings.
4 Make a wish	Reading of part 1 of 'King Midas'. Discussing story themes.	Identifying speech marks and discussing their purpose. Reading dialogue aloud.	Writing a dialogue and preparing to perform it.	Writing a dialogue and preparing to perform it.	Performing dialogues. Noting story language and speech marks.
5 What happens next?	Predicting story ending and writing answers about King Midas.	Learning to spell words that begin with the digraph **wh**.	Answering questions about the story in complete sentences.	Answering questions about the story in complete sentences.	Answering questions as a class and discussing them.

UNIT 4

Hour	Shared text level work	Shared word/ sentence level work	Guided reading/ writing	Independent work	Plenary
6 The character of Kind Midas	Reading the final part of the story. Discussing character traits and compiling character webs.	Learning about words with the prefixes *un-* and *dis-*.	Using the character web to write descriptive sentences.	Making character webs about King Midas.	Sharing character webs. Holding a quiz of modifying words with *un-* or *dis-*.
7 Retelling the story	Recalling story events. Adapting story for performance..	Writing notes to adapt text.	Preparing to retell story through drama.	Preparing to retell story through drama.	Retelling the story in performance.
8 What do you think?	Reading 'King Log and King Stork' and discussing characters.	Looking at words with an *er* sound in them. Learning how to add this as a suffix to show an increase or decrease in amount.	Writing sentences about the story using *er* words. Discussing words with *er* sound but different spellings.	Writing sentences about the story using *er* words.	Sharing sentences about the story. Looking at other ways of making the *er* sound.
9 Missing words	Begin retelling the story.	Completing cloze sentences.	Completing a version of the story by filling in missing words.	Completing a version of the story by filling in missing words.	Reading the incomplete story and discussing words which could be used to complete it.
10 All three stories	Creating a chart of themes, characters and settings in the three stories.	Writing sentences based on information from the table.	Answering questions about the three stories. Discussing other aspects they could write about.	Answering questions about the three stories.	Discussing the children's views on the three stories.

Key assessment opportunities
● Can the children describe themes, settings and characters?
● Could they predict endings and retell stories?
● Can they write simple sentences?
● Do they understand the use of speech marks?
● Can they spell words containing er and beginning with wh, un and dis?

UNIT 4 HOUR 1 Narrative 2

Story themes

Objectives

NLS
T7: To prepare and retell stories individually and through role play.
S6: To identify speech marks in reading, understand their purpose, use the terms correctly.

S&L
16 Drama: To adopt appropriate roles in small or large groups.

What you need
● Photocopiable page 113.

Shared text-level work
● Read part 1 of 'The Thick Fat Pancake'. Then discuss the story and ask the children to recount the events so far. Ask:

> Where is the story set?
> What problem did the mother face? How did she try to solve the problem?
> What did the children think about the enormous pancake?
> What did the pancake think about being eaten?
> How do you know that this is not a true story?

● Discuss answers and talk about the theme of the story and other stories with a similar theme, for example 'The Gingerbread Man'.

Shared sentence-level work
● Look at the section of the story where seven children make statements about the pancake. Ask seven children to read the speech out clearly and with expression and intonation, reminding them that they should only say words inside the speech marks. Ask the rest of the class to read text not in the speech marks.
● Note how the speech is punctuated and how an exclamation mark or question mark indicates how the words are said.

Guided and independent work
● Re-read the text. Show how to use phonological, contextual and grammatical clues to work out unfamiliar words and make sense of what is read. For example, the word *Norway* may be unfamiliar. If they look at the grammar, the children can see that the word follows *in* and has a capital letter, so it must be a place. If they break the word into its syllables, they should be able to pronounce it.
● Ask the children to re-read the story in pairs, then go on to look at the speech from the seven children in the story and then find the next piece of speech. Ask them to think about the words that the children and the pancake spoke and then join into groups to practise saying the lines with expression and appropriate intonation.
● You could have groups of nine so that each role is played by one person, or you may wish to involve children more by having some playing more than one role. Encourage the children to discuss the way in which the lines should be spoken and to prepare to perform them for the whole class in the plenary. Consider providing each group with a tape recorder so they can record their dialogue to play to the class in the plenary.

Plenary
● Ask the children to present their pieces of dialogue. Encourage others to give constructive comments.
● Write some examples on the board and draw attention to the placement of speech marks.

Differentiation

Less able
● Encourage children to extend the dialogue so that each character has at least two lines to say.

More able
● Children may need to work with others to read the text and say their lines appropriately. If adult support is not available, group them with better readers.

Predicting the ending

Objectives

NLS
T4: To predict story endings/incidents, eg from unfinished extracts, while reading with the teacher.
W5: To discriminate, orally, syllables in multi-syllabic words.

What you need
● Photocopiable page 113.

Shared text-level work
● Ask the children to recall the story from the previous lesson. Then re-read the text with them.
● Focus on the last sentence and ask for predictions of what may happen next. List ideas on the board. For example:

> Where do you think the pancake might roll next?
> How/where will it stop rolling?
> Do you think the children will catch up with it and eat it?
> Who else might be involved in this part of the story?

● Ask the children to help you to write the second half of the story. Work together to use the list of ideas in the first few sentences. Encourage them to include dialogue if appropriate, and show them how this can be written.
● As you write, say what you are doing when, for example, you use a full stop, comma or capital letter, and talk about spellings:

> I want to write, 'The pancake rolled past the farm dog,', so I'll need to begin the sentence with a capital letter; the pancake is 'pan' and 'cake'; I need to write 'rolled', so that's 'roll' with an '-ed' at the end; and at the end of the sentence I need a full stop, or should I use an exclamation mark?

● Leave the list and sentences on the board as a starting point for independent work.

Shared word-level work
● Talk about some of the longer words in the first part of the story and in the shared list and sentences, for example *Norway, pancake, rolled, special, eaten, caught, catch.* Say the words and point to the letters that represent the sounds. Show how words may be broken down into syllables to aid pronunciation and decoding.
● Go on to look at some of the other multi-syllabic words in the story (for example *wonderful, golden, enormous*) and ask the children to break these into syllables before re-reading them.

Guided and independent work
● Ask the children to work in pairs to write their version of the next part of the story. Encourage them to make use of the list on the board to guide their story structure, but to include their own ideas if they can. Remind them to check spellings and to re-read their story regularly.
● Stop the children periodically to read their work aloud and discuss spellings and use of story language.

Plenary
● Share the stories and discuss different events and any new characters and settings introduced. Are there many variations? Have some groups come up with the same ideas?

Differentiation

Less able
● Ask children to produce their stories in note form and with pictures.

More able
● Let children choose how to structure their stories.

Objectives

NLS
T3: To discuss and compare story themes.
S5: To use verb tenses with increasing accuracy in speaking and writing.

What you need

● Photocopiable pages 113 and 114.

Differentiation

Less able
● Underline the verbs in the sentences. If necessary, provide a list of the verbs in their past tense form to choose from.

More able
● Ask children to write more sentences in the present tense for writing partners to change into the past tense.

Comparing the endings

Shared text-level work

● Ask the children to remind each other about what had happened at the end of part 1, and recall their versions of the story ending.
● Explain that now they are going to find out how the published version ends. Read and discuss part 2. Ask the children which version they prefer and why.
● Talk about the concluding paragraph that suggests that all piglets sniff the ground because they are hoping to find the rest of the pancake. Do the children think this is true? Explain that there are many stories that suggest explanations for a particular phenomenon. Ask if they can think of any, and encourage them to find out from adults at home if they know any. (For example, Rudyard Kipling's 'Just So' stories like 'How the Leopard Got his Spots', 'How the Elephant Got his Trunk' and 'How the Camel Got his Hump'.)

Shared sentence-level work

● Talk about the fact that the verbs in the story are in the past tense. Look in particular at *rolled, reached, stopped, flipped* and *jumped.*
● For comparison, say some phrases with these words in the present tense, such as *I roll down the hillside; I reach up to the top shelf.* Ask the children to change the tense of the phrases.
● Identify the *-ed* suffix which is used in regular verbs, but point out that some words, such as *catch* and *go*, do not have this ending. Discuss the past tense forms of common irregular verbs.
● Note that not all verbs in a story are in the past tense. For example, in the final paragraph the narrator switches to the present. This is characteristic of story writing, and non-fiction, when something is being concluded or explained. Find further examples of this to show to the children in future lessons.

Guided and independent work

● Support one group as they attempt photocopiable page 114. If they cope well, provide them with further sentences which include more verbs with irregular past tenses.
● Ask the group to find further examples of past-tense verbs in their reading books.
● Encourage children to work on photocopiable page 114 individually.

Plenary

● Ask children to suggest further sentences in the present tense for the class to change into the past tense orally. Write examples on the board where there are misconceptions or where the spellings of verbs are irregular.
● Make a display of verbs in the present and past tense, with words on individual cards which children can match up.
● Play a matching pairs game with verbs and their past tenses, where children must turn over one card and then find its past or present tense.

UNIT 4 HOUR 4 📖 Narrative 2

Make a wish

Objectives

NLS
T3: To discuss and compare story themes.
S6: To identify speech marks in reading, understand their purpose, use the terms correctly.

What you need
● Photocopiable page 115.

Shared text-level work
● Read part 1 of this story. Explain that the Ancient Greeks believed in many gods and that it was one of these gods who is supposed to have visited Midas.
● Talk about the events in this part of the story and ask the children if they know of other stories in which people make wishes. ('Rapunzel', 'The Three Wishes', 'Snow White'.). Ask if the people who have their wishes granted are always happier afterwards. For example, in 'The Three Wishes' the couple end up no wealthier than when they started, but they do learn a lesson about life.
● Let the children discuss in pairs what they would ask for if they were granted a wish. Ask the children to share their partners' ideas with the class. Talk about how their lives might change if their wishes were granted.

Shared sentence-level work
● Focus on the section of dialogue, asking two good readers to play the roles. Remind the children how the speech marks separate speech from other text.
● Now ask the children to work in pairs to practise reading the dialogue out loud.
● Encourage some pairs to read the dialogue while the class reads all the words that are not speech.

Guided and independent work
● Ask children to write a short conversation between themselves and someone they meet who offers to grant them a wish. Encourage them to use speech marks if they can. Help them to get started by brainstorming ideas and writing an example opening on the board:

> One day, I was sitting in my room, when a lady in a beautiful blue gown suddenly appeared in front of me.
> 'You've been a very well-behaved child,' she said. 'As a reward I am going to grant you one wish. You may choose anything you like.'

● Ask the children to work in pairs to work through ideas orally and take turns to write the lines. Ask the pairs to practise reading ready for the plenary.

Differentiation

Less able
● Ask children to record their conversations on tape.

More able
● Create mixed-ability pairings so that one child might help with writing.

Plenary
● Ask some of the pairs to perform their dialogues.
● Discuss the language they have used, focusing on the effect this has on the quality of the story for those listening. For example, which words and phrases do children use to express excitement, wonder or surprise?
● Write some extracts of their work, asking the children to tell you where to put speech marks.
● Ask children to think about what might happen once the wish is granted. Can they think of good and bad outcomes?

What happens next?

Objectives

NLS
T4: To predict story endings/incidents, eg from unfinished extracts, while reading with the teacher.
S9: To secure the use of simple sentences in own writing.
W3: To read and spell words containing the digraph *wh*.

What you need
- Photocopiable pages 115 and 116
- dictionaries.

Shared text-level work
- Re-read the first part of the King Midas story and ask the children to think about what might happen next. Remind them that Midas is about to have his dinner.
- Write on the board, with sufficient space for an answer after each, a series of questions about the story, each beginning with a *wh* word. These might include:

  - Where does the story take place?
  - When did the story take place?
  - Who is the story about?
  - Why did Midas want everything he owned to be made of gold?
  - What will happen when he touches his food?

- Ask the children to help you to answer the questions and write the answers in complete sentences. Look at some of the words beginning with wh, such as when, where, why, who, which often begin sentences. Talk about the importance of placing a question mark at the end of a question to help the reader to understand how to read it and what it means. For example:

  Where did the story take place?
  > *The story took place in Greece.*
  When did the story take place?
  > *The story is set many hundreds of years ago.*

- Model the sentence-writing for the children. Make deliberate mistakes for them to spot and correct, such as missing out capital letters or full stops, or writing just short phrases or one-word answers.
- Discuss with the children what they think might happen next and encourage them to share their predictions with partners.

Shared word-level work
- Help the children to learn to spell the *wh* words. Ask them to use simple dictionaries to find further words which begin with *wh* for you to write on the board, such as *wheel, whack, white, whose,* and *whole*.

Guided and independent work
- Show the children photocopiable page 116, which presents a series of questions about the rest of the story. Ask them to read the questions and then work in small groups to discuss and then answer each one.
- Note that some of the questions begin with *wh* words, but others do not. Identify *how* as common word that often begins a question.
- Remind the children to write their answers as complete sentences.

Differentiation

Less able
- Provide good readers and writers for each table, but expect all children to discuss answers.

More able
- Children could go on to write additional questions.

Plenary
- Ask children to share their answers and help you to write them in sentences on an enlarged version of the photocopiable sheet.
- Explain that there are many possible answers to the questions.

The character of King Midas

Objectives

NLS
T6: To identify and describe characters, expressing own views and using words and phrases from texts.
W8: To spell words with common prefixes, eg *un-* and *dis-*, to indicate the negative.

What you need
● Photocopiable page 115
● dictionaries and thesauruses.

Shared text-level work
● Read part 2 of the story. Discuss the events and the ending, and ask the children to compare it with their ideas when they answered the questions in the previous lesson.
● Focus on the ending and ask the children if they are satisfied with it. Do they think that Midas *has* learned a lesson? Do they think he should have been given the chance to return to normal?
● Write *King Midas* in the centre of the board and ask the children to think about him as a character. Ask them to suggest words and phrases that describe him. Write several of these on the board so that a character web emerges. Encourage the children to refer to the text to back up their ideas.

Shared word-level work
● Write the words *happy* and *unhappy*, and *like* and *dislike* on the board. Ask the children for phrases or sentences to describe Midas which include these words. Look at any words from the character web which include the prefixes *un-* or *dis-* or which could be modified by adding them, for example *unpleasant, unkind, displeased*.
● Focus on the words *happy* and *unhappy*, and *like* and *dislike,* and ask the children if they can explain what adding the prefixes *un-* or *dis-* does to the meaning of a word. Show them other examples such as *kind* and *unkind, pleased* and *displeased* to reinforce the concept that the prefixes create negatives and opposites (antonyms).

Guided and independent work
● Discuss with a group ways in which they could expand single words and phrases to create sentences about King Midas. Begin with words from the character web and ask the children to suggest sentences which could include them.
● Encourage the children to think of words that begin with the prefixes *un-* and *dis-* and let them use simple dictionaries to find examples.
● Ask the children to make their own character webs for King Midas and explain that this will help them later when they retell the story.
● Stop the children occasionally to discuss ideas, and take the opportunity to practise correct spellings on the board for some of the suggested words suggested.

Differentiation

Less able
● Ask children to use words from the character web and to use it to help their spellings. Encourage them to add to the words in the web.

More able
● Let children use thesauruses to expand the vocabulary in their webs.

Plenary
● Ask each pair to show their character webs to another pair and to discuss them. Then ask the groups of four to report back on good ideas to the whole class. Write these on the board and go over spellings and meanings.
● Write words on the board which can be modified using *un-* or *dis-* and ask children to tell you which prefix to use. This could be done in a quiz format, with teams taking turns to discuss and then provide the answers. Devise a points system for the game and encourage all children to contribute.

Retelling the story

Objectives

NLS
T7: To prepare and retell stories individually and through role-play in groups, using dialogue and narrative from text.

S&L
17 Speaking: To tell real and imagined stories using the conventions of familiar story language.
24 Drama: To present parts of traditional stories for members of their class.

What you need
● Photocopiable page 115
● completed photocopiable page 116.

Shared text-level work
● In this lesson, the children will be acting out their story endings. They will almost certainly need more time than is available in one hour, so make additional time if possible.
● Read the whole of 'King Midas' to the children, inviting them to join in. Ask children to play the roles of Midas, the god and Marigold and to speak their lines expressively.
● When you have read the story, ask the children to recall the key events of part 1. List these on the board, for example:

> Midas was very rich.
> He wanted to be even richer.
> A god visited him in his garden.
> Midas wishes that everything he had could be turned to gold.

● Explain to the children that they will be able to use the list and the character webs they produced in the previous lesson to help them to produce and perform their own version of the story. Ask them to discuss in small groups how they might perform the story.
● Draw upon the children's ideas to write a story opening with them. Emphasise that the children do not have to use this opening if they have better ideas, but that they may if it helps them to get started.

Shared sentence-level work
● Explain to the children that they will need to make brief notes to remind them of the order of events and of who needs to say what and when. Show them how they can do this by writing some notes on the board. For example:

> Midas touches things: fence, flower, knife and fork – all turn to gold. Daughter turns to gold.

● Explain that the notes need only be brief and should act as reminders of what actors will need to do in the same way that a shopping list or a to do list helps us to remember things.

Guided and independent work
● Ask the children to retell the whole story if possible, working in pairs to make notes and then act it out.

Plenary
● Ask the children to act out the stories. If they have not had time to prepare a performance of the whole story, they could perform the parts that they have prepared.
● Encourage them to consider their audience.
● Talk about the stories they have performed and explain that if they are not yet finished, you will provide extra time for children to complete their stories.

Differentiation

Less able
● Support a lower ability group who need help with making notes and stop them occasionally to discuss these. Help them to prepare their performance.
● Some children may spend most of their time acting the story, but encourage them to make notes on the sequence of events.

More able
● Encourage the children to use a greater range of vocabulary.

UNIT 4 HOUR 8 ▢ Narrative 2

Objectives

NLS
T1: To reinforce and apply their word-level skills through shared and guided reading.
W2: To learn the common spelling patterns for the vowel phoneme er.

What you need
● Photocopiable page 117.

What do you think?

Shared text-level work
● Read the story with the children, helping with difficult words.
● Find out the children's understanding of and feelings about the story. What do they like or dislike?
● Discuss the setting and characters. What do they think about King Log? What do they think about the frogs? Were they sensible to want a king and did they go about choosing one sensibly?

Shared word-level work
● Write on the board winter, after, better, over and never. Ask the children what they notice. Discuss the common er ending and ask how the letters are sounded together.
● Now ask them to look at the story and try to find the words in it.
● Talk about other words that include er and have the er sound as in her. Help the children by writing words connected with size and amounts (big, tall, short, high, low, fat, thin and so on) and asking them to add an -er suffix to show an increase or decrease in size.
● Note any changes that occur when a suffix is added. For example, big gets an extra g when it becomes bigger, fat gets an extra t when it becomes fatter.
● Ask the children to see if they can find other words in the story with the er sound as in her. These need not necessarily have er at the end, and might include perhaps, interferes, were, water, wonderful and answered. Add these to the list on the board.
● It may be necessary to talk about the pronunciation in serious and very and the second er in interferes.

Guided and independent work
● Ask the children to use the list of er words to write sentences related to the story. Each sentence should include an er word and focus on events in the story and their opinions about them. Encourage them to work in pairs to support each other with spellings and sentences, as well as ideas.
● After writing sentences, discuss other words that have an er sound made using different combinations of letters, for example, word, heard, bird and blurred.

Plenary
● Ask volunteers to read out their sentences. Ask other children to identify the er word each time and to write it on the board. Check the spellings as a class.
● Ask the guided group to introduce words that have an er sound made by other letters. Write some of these on the board and ask the rest of the class if they can think of any more. Suggest that they try to find some more of these words in dictionaries, reminding them of how to use the dictionary.
● Make a display of words which include an er sound and encourage children to add to this as they discover new words.

Differentiation

Less able
Provide partially completed sentences for children so that they can add er words to complete them.

More able
● Give children word, heard, bird and blurred as headings, and ask them to find other words with similar spellings for the er sound.

Objectives

NLS
T2: To use phonological, contextual, grammatical and graphic knowledge to work out, predict and check the meanings of unfamiliar words and to make sense of what they read.
S1: To use awareness of grammar to decipher new or unfamiliar words, eg to predict from the text, read on, leave a gap and re-read.

What you need

● Photocopiable pages 117 and 118.

Missing words

Shared text-level work

● Re-read the story and explain to the children that they are going to help you to start a class version of the story.
● Using the children's ideas, write an opening sentence for the story. Talk about the ways in which traditional tales often begin and ask the children to think of a line which sets the scene for the story and makes the reader want to read on.
● Next, write a suitable following sentence, but include a space where you miss out a word. For example, *The frogs decided that they ___ a king to rule over them*. Ask the children to read the sentence and see if they can spot the 'mistake'.
● Ask them to choose the right word to fill the space. Suggest they read on beyond the missing word to use as many clues as possible. They might suggest *wanted, needed* or even two words such as *would like*. Emphasise that there are many different correct answers, but the word should be the same part of speech (noun, verb and so on) and the sentence should make sense grammatically and fit in the story. Re-read the sentence to check.

Shared sentence-level work

● Go on to write further sentences for the retelling of the story, each time missing a word or words out and asking the children to help you to complete them.
● Challenge children to work in pairs to make up sentences with missing words, ideally about the story. (They could use mini whiteboards.) Write some of these on the board for the class to complete. Emphasise that there are many different correct answers, and praise children who make descriptive choices.

Guided and independent work

● Provide pairs of children with photocopiable page 118 and ask them to read the whole of the text before attempting to fill in the spaces with appropriate words. Encourage children to discuss and justify their choices.
● Emphasise that in many cases the spaces could be filled with one from a variety of words. For example, *pond, pool* and *lake* would all be suitable for the first space; *king, ruler* and *leader* could be appropriate for the second. The important thing is that the children use the grammar and semantics of the text to help them.
● Guide one group to support the children as they complete the sheet and discuss possible word choices with them.

Plenary

● Re-read the text aloud to the class and pause at the end of sentences that have missing words to ask children for their suggestions. Again, explain that there is not necessarily one correct word which will fit each space, and praise imaginative and interesting suggestions that fit grammatically.

Differentiation

Less able
● Provide a list of words that could fit the spaces. Read through the list with them first
● Ensure that more able readers can help each table.

More able
● Ask children to go on to write their own incomplete sentences for each other to complete.

All three stories

Objectives

NLS
T3: To discuss and compare story themes.
T5: To discuss story settings.
T6: To identify and describe characters.
S9: To secure the use of simple sentences in own writing.

S&L
18 Listening: To respond to presentations by describing characters, repeating some highlights and commenting constructively.

What you need
● Photocopiable pages 113–118.

Shared text-level work
● This final lesson provides an opportunity to assess children's appreciation of story settings, themes and characters, as well as their ability to write in sentences.
● Recap the stories from this unit.
● Ask them to tell you the titles of the stories. Write these on the board as column headings:

	The thick, fat pancake	King Midas	King Log and King Stork
Setting			
Characters			
Theme			

● Ask the children to discuss in pairs the settings for each of the stories. Share ideas, then write their answers in the chart in note form.
● Identify the characters. Ask the children to suggest an adjective for each character or group of characters. Add this information to the chart.
● Finally, ask the children to think about the themes of each story. Make suggestions for some well-known stories, without first telling the children which stories you are describing. For the three stories in this unit they might suggest:

> A natural phenomenon is explained through a story ('The Thick Fat Pancake').
> A greedy king learns a lesson ('King Midas').
> Doing nothing is better than doing the wrong thing ('King Log and King Stork').

Shared word- and sentence-level work
● Ask the children to help you to write sentences based upon the chart. Demonstrate how to expand notes into sentences, pointing out the use of capital letters and full stops.

Guided and independent work
● Ask the children to work individually to answer these questions:
  1. Which story did you like best and why?
  2. Which character did you like best in the three stories and why?
  3. Which character did you like least and why?
  4. Which story had the best ending and why?
  5. Write about another aspect of the stories which interested you.

Differentiation

Less able
● Ask children to answer the first four questions only.

More able
● Encourage children to comment on other aspects of the stories.

● Tell them to write at least one sentence for each question and to make reference to the texts in their answers.
● Support a group as they write their answers, and discuss what 'further aspects' of the stories they could write sentences about.

Plenary
● Go through the questions one at a time with the class.
● Discuss the children's choices for favourite story and for favourite and least favourite character. Encourage them to justify their choices by referring to the stories and each other's evaluations.

The Thick Fat Pancake

Part 1

A woman who lived in Norway had seven children. They were always hungry. Their favourite food was pancakes, and they always argued about who should get the first pancake.

One day their mother was fed up with all the arguing, so she decided to cook one great big thick fat pancake for all the children to share.

So she took a big bag of flour and a box of eggs and a jug of milk and some salt, and mixed up a bowlful of creamy batter. She melted some butter in her largest frying pan, and poured all the batter in at once, so that the biggest, thickest, fattest pancake you can imagine was soon sizzling in the pan. The children gathered round.

The first child said, "It looks wonderful!"

The second child said, "It smells delicious!"

The third child said, "It's so golden!"

The fourth child said, "It's so enormous!"

The fifth child said, "It's the best pancake ever!"

The sixth child said, "It's nearly ready!"

And the seventh child said, "Where's my spoon and fork?"

When it heard this, the pancake said to itself, "Spoon and fork? Oh no! I am much too special to be eaten by these children." It jumped out of the pan and went roly-poly-roly out of the door and off down the road. The children ran after it, but it rolled too fast to be caught.

Part 2

The thick fat pancake rolled past the farm dog, past the goat and the chickens. It rolled too fast for the cow to lick it, or the ducks to peck it, or the sheep to nibble it. It rolled on over the fields until it reached the river. There the pancake stopped.

A pink piglet who had been chasing it came up and said, "Thick fat pancake, would you like a lift across the river?"

"Yes please!" said the pancake, and flipped itself up onto the piglet's snout.

The piglet set off paddling to the other side, but when he was nearly there, he suddenly went "Snap!" and took a bite out of the pancake. The pancake leapt high and far, and landed on the riverbank. It rolled away over the hills and out of sight.

And that is why piglets are always sniffing with their snouts on the ground – they are still hoping to find the rest of that thick fat pancake.

Rosemary Waugh

Telling it like it was

■ These sentences about the story are in the present tense, as if they are happening now. Rewrite them in the past tense to show that they happened some time ago.

1. The woman and her children live in Norway.

2. The children are always hungry.

3. Mother mixes all the ingredients in a bowl.

4. She cooks a great big pancake.

5. The children want to eat the pancake.

6. The pancake rolls away.

7. The children chase after it.

8. The animals all try to eat the pancake.

9. A piglet helps the pancake to cross the river.

10. The piglet tries to eat the pancake, but the pancake rolls away.

King Midas

Part 1

Once, long ago, there was a Greek king called Midas. He was very rich. He lived in a beautiful grand palace with beautiful gardens, and he had the very best of everything to eat and drink.

However, Midas was never quite satisfied. He kept thinking of how he could become even richer. One day, when he was walking in his garden, a god visited him.

"King Midas! You don't look happy," said the god.

"How can I be happy," replied Midas, "when there is gold going into the pockets of other men?"

"Is gold so important?" asked the god.

"Of course it is! Gold is the most important thing in the world! I wish that everything I had was made of gold – then I would be truly happy," said Midas.

"Well, you shall have your wish", said the god. "From now on, everything you touch will turn to gold, and we shall see if it makes you happy." Then the god disappeared.

Midas reached out and touched the fence. At once it turned from wood into gold. He picked a flower, and found that he was holding a flower of gold. It no longer had its lovely scent and delicate colours. Still, Midas was feeling very pleased and excited as he went in to dinner.

Part 2

King Midas picked up his knife and fork – which, of course, turned to gold in his hands, and when the food reached his lips he could not bite or chew it because it too had turned to gold.

Just as Midas was worrying about this, the door opened and his daughter Marigold came running in. "Father!" she called. "Look what I've found!" Midas held out his arms to hug her.

As soon as he touched her, she became a shining golden statue.

Midas was horrified and heartbroken. "What have I done!" he cried. "If only I had never made such a silly wish!"

Suddenly the god appeared beside him. "Well, Midas," he said. "Do you still think gold is the best thing in the world?"

"No, indeed," said Midas sadly. "I can see how foolish and greedy I was."

The god was sorry for him, and turned Marigold, and everything else Midas had touched, back to the way they were.

Never again did Midas complain that he wanted more gold.

Rosemary Waugh

TERM 2

The ending of the King Midas story

◼ Answer these questions about the story. Write full sentences.

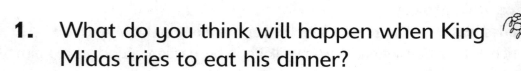

1. What do you think will happen when King Midas tries to eat his dinner?

_____

_____

_____

2. In the next part of the story King Midas sees his daughter. What do you think might happen?

_____

_____

_____

3. Do you think Midas will be happy making everything turn to gold?

_____

_____

_____

4. What else do you think will happen in the story?

_____

_____

_____

5. How do you think the story will end?

_____

_____

_____

ALL NEW 100 LITERACY HOURS · YEAR 2

◤**SCHOLASTIC**

King Log and King Stork

Avery long time ago, a group of frogs lived in a muddy pond in a meadow. One day, they decided that they should choose a king to rule over them, because they were always arguing. Of course, the very next thing they did was to argue about which of them should be king. In the end, one of them said, "Since we can't agree on who should be king, let's not choose one of ourselves. Look at that log on the other side of the pond. He never interferes when we fall out. He never argues, but is always quiet and serious. Let's make him our king!"

The other frogs agreed, and they went and told the log that it was now King Log. The log said nothing. It did nothing.

When the rain flooded the pond all over the field, King Log did nothing. When winter froze the water to ice, and the frogs could not find food, King Log did nothing. When the summer sun dried the pond to a tiny puddle, King Log did nothing.

At last the frogs decided that the log was a bad king who did nothing to help them. "Let's choose a new king!" they said. "Who shall it be?" Just then a tall stork flew down to the pond. The frogs all admired the big bird, with his long legs and graceful wings. "The stork would be a wonderful king!" they agreed, and they called out to him, "Stork! We have chosen you to be our king!"

"Your king, am I?" said the stork. "Does that mean I can rule over you?"

"Yes", answered the frogs. "We are tired of a king who does nothing. We want a king who will do important things for us!"

"Thank you!" said the stork, and, leaning his long sharp beak down into the pond, he gobbled up the silly frogs.

Perhaps King Log, who did nothing, was, after all, a better king than King Stork turned out to be!

Rosemary Waugh

Missing words

◼ Read the story carefully. Decide which words to put in the spaces.

Many years ago some frogs, who lived in a muddy
_____ in a meadow, wanted to choose a
_____ . They argued about who should be king.
In the _____ , they decided that it would be best
not to have a frog as king, so they looked around for
someone _____ to be their ruler.

   The frogs saw a log at the side of the _____
and decided that it would make a good king. When they
told the log it was their king, it did not _____
anything or _____ anything.

   For many months the log did _____ , even
when the pond flooded or froze or dried up. The frogs
decided they needed a _____ who would help
them, so they looked around for someone else.

   A large stork flew
over the pond and the
frogs decided that he
would _____
a perfect king. They
told the stork he was
their king and the stork
thanked them. Then he
dipped his long, sharp
beak into the
_____ and
ate all the frogs.

UNIT 5 ▭

Explanation

This unit investigates different ways in which to present texts, including lists, flow charts and simple descriptive sentences. It will help children to develop their understanding of and ability to use lists and flow charts, as well as enabling them to learn to spell dates and months of the year. The activities can be linked to work in maths, geography and science where flow charts and cycles are used, and history, where sequences of events are studied. This unit also covers *Progression in phonics*, step 7.

Hour	Shared text-level work	Shared word-/ sentence-level work	Guided work	Independent work	Plenary
1 Birthdays	Writing about the children's birthdays, focusing on days and dates.	Spelling months of the year and children's names. Using information gathered to write sentences.	Writing simple sentences about birthdays.	Writing simple sentences about information in a table.	Sharing sentences and learning to spell months of the year.
2 Months of the year	Creating a cyclical flow chart of the months of the year.	Learning to sound and spell months of the year.	Producing flow chart of months with notes about birthdays and events.	Producing flow chart of months with notes about birthdays and events.	Using children's ideas to create a class flow chart. Revising spelling of months.
3 My celebration	Reading about preparations for a birthday party.	Using speech marks and speech verbs to identify and read out dialogue.	Writing different types of list for celebration preparations.	Writing list for celebration preparations.	Sharing lists and looking at different ways of presenting them.
4 Flow charts	Reading a flow chart about organising a birthday party.	Discussing information in the chart. Learning ordinal numbers.	Writing simple sentences related to the flow chart. Looking at other flow charts.	Writing simple sentences about the flow chart.	Writing answers as a class. Revising new words.
5 Birthday present	Writing to produce a flow chart of preparations for a birthday party.	Looking at different ways of presenting text.	Creating flow charts using a list of points.	Creating flow charts using a list of points.	Comparing layouts of charts. Reviewing the unit.

Key assessment opportunities
● Can children spell the months of the year? Do they understand the order in which they appear?
● Can they follow and create flow charts?
● Can they use sequential words?
● Do they write in sentences.

Birthdays

Shared text-level work

● Check the register to find out which children have recently had birthdays and who will have them in the next few weeks. Prepare some sentences about these children's birthdays and display them on the board. For example, *Kate's birthday is on 10 February. Sarah's birthday was on 3 February. Jamal's birthday is tomorrow.*

● Talk about the use of abbreviations when giving dates in numbers and words (2nd, 3rd, 4th, 21st...) and explain that you will be looking at these in more detail later.

● Read the sentences, asking the children who feature in them to tell you something about their birthday, perhaps details about a celebration, or how old they were/will be.

● Use this information to write further sentences on the board or extend the existing ones. For example, *Sarah's birthday was on 3 February and she had a party. Jamal's will be seven tomorrow.*

Shared word-level work

● Practise the spellings of the months of the year, writing them on the board.

● Ask the children to tell you in which month they have their birthday. (Have the register handy in case some are not sure.) Write the children's names next to the months to produce a table. For example:

Month	Children's birthdays
January	Chloe, Ellie, Ben
February	Kate, Sarah, Jack
March	Tom, William, Naseem, Jessica

Shared sentence-level work

● Write a simple sentence about information in the table, for example *Kate, Sarah and Jack have birthdays in February*. Write further sentences suggested by the children.

● Practise writing dates by asking children to write, for example, their birthday or today's date or yesterday's date on the board.

Guided and independent work

● Help children to write sentences about their birthdays and those of friends/family. For example, *My birthday is on 20 July and I will be seven. My friend Callum's birthday is on 6 October.*

Plenary

● Share some of the children's sentences on the board. Praise clear, informative sentences.

● Emphasise the importance of beginning sentences with capital letters and ending them with full stops.

● Show the children how they can learn the months using Look>Say>Cover>Write>Check.

● Focus on *February* and look at the r after the b and at the *-uary* ending. Pay particular attention to tricky bits when learning spellings.

Months of the year

Objectives

NLS
T2: To use phonological, contextual, grammatical and graphic knowledge to work out, predict and check the meanings of unfamiliar words.
W6: To read on sight and spell all the words from Appendix List 1.

What you need
● List of the months of the year
● months of the year on individual cards (several of each).

Shared text-level work
● Read the months of the year with the children.
● Hold up the cards at random, asking children to tell you if their birthdays are in the months that you hold up. Hand those children the appropriate cards.
● When all the cards have been distributed, ask which is the first month of the year. Attach *January* to the top left of the board and draw an arrow across to a space for the second month. Ask which is the second month, and place *February* at the end of the arrow.
● Repeat this until all of the months are on the board and a square or circular flow chart has been created, with an arrow from December back to January.
● Show the children the cyclical nature of the flow chart and ask them to explain why there is an arrow from December to January.

Shared word-level work
● Practise the spellings of the months. Sound the words *January* and *February* in syllables. Be careful with February as the last two syllables are often squashed and the first r isn't always pronounced. For *March*, note the consonant digraph *ch*. For *April*, note the long initial A (rather than short a as in *at*). For *August*, focus on the initial vowel digraph *Au* and relate this to other words such as *author, autumn* and *automatic*. Split *September, October, November* and *December* into syllables and tell the children that the prefixes relate to the numbers seven, eight, nine and ten. Explain that there were ten months in the year until the Romans introduced July and August, named after Julius Caesar and Augustus Caesar.
● Remind the children that the names of the months, like the days of the week, always begin with a capital letter.

Guided and independent work
● Provide each child or pair with a large sheet of paper and smaller pieces on which they can write details for a flow chart 'calendar'.
● Discuss each month in turn and ask for ideas for what to write about it, such as *January is the first month of the year. February is the shortest month*. The children need only write brief notes. For example:

> **August**
> Summer holidays
> Eighth month
> Named after Augustus Caesar

● Ask the children to arrange and stick their pieces of paper onto the larger sheet as a flow chart.

Plenary
● Ask for details to add to a flow chart calendar on the board.
● Ask the children spell the months of the year.

Differentiation

Less able
● If children find the writing difficult, provide some sample phrases as models.

More able
● Provide access to a computer so that children can create a cyclical flow chart and print it out.

UNIT 5 HOUR 3 ▭ Explanation

My celebration

Objectives

NLS
T21: To produce simple flow charts that explain a process.
S6: To identify speech marks in reading, understand their purpose, use the terms correctly.
S7: To investigate and recognise a range of other ways of presenting texts.

What you need
● Photocopiable page 125.

Shared text-level work
● Read 'My birthday party' with the children.
● Encourage the children to relate it to their own experience by talking briefly about parties they have had or been to.
● Talk about the characteristics of the list: short, simple sentences, numbered to show a sequence.
● Re-read the list and ask the children if they can think of other things to do. Compile a list of key words and phrases on the board, such as *decorate, prize, tidy, cake, games, invitations* and *candles*.
● Identify the three different types of text within 'My birthday party': dialogue, list, and narrative. Draw attention to the dialogue at the beginning, which might be typical of a story; then look at the list, which is written concisely and in note/instruction form. Finally, look at the last paragraph, set out in narrative form.
● Discuss the different text types and note examples of where each type is usually found.

Shared sentence-level work
● Ask two good readers to read the words spoken by Mum and the child, with the rest of the class reading the narration in the first paragraph.
● Ask the children how they could tell which were the words spoken and to point out the speech marks.
● Talk about the verb *said*, and discuss alternatives such as *cried, called, shouted* and *whispered*.

Guided and independent work
● Support one group, talking about spellings and ways of phrasing their writing. Give guidance about writing a list and talk about lists that are sequential and might be numbered, as well as those that tend to be more random, such as shopping lists.
● Ask the children to make a list of their own for another celebration. This could be for a religious occasion or a special outing to the cinema or a restaurant. Encourage them to discuss their ideas in pairs and make each item brief.
● Ask children to keep a record of any word which they do not know how to spell. Suggest that they note down the meaning of the word and write a sentence that uses it.

Differentiation
Less able
● Ask children to write to a set format.

More able
● Provide access to computers. Encourage children to use the spell checker as well as to experiment with formats.

Plenary
● Write examples of the children's lists on the board and check phrasing and spelling.
● Discuss how children have presented their lists. Have they all numbered them? Have some used bullet points? Have they placed items underneath each other? Explain that there are many ways of presenting a list. Talk about other lists the children may know, such as the school register, shopping lists, birthday/Christmas wish-lists, school/class rules.

Flow charts

Objectives

NLS
T19: To read flow charts that explain a process.
S7: To investigate and recognise a range of other ways of presenting texts.
W10: To learn new words from reading linked to particular topics.

What you need
● Photocopiable pages 126 and 127
● examples of similar flow charts

Shared text-level work
● Remind the children of their lists, and explain that they will be looking at another way of presenting a series of events.
● Ask the children to tell you about the order of a sequence of actions for a common activity such as cleaning your teeth or making a glass of orange squash. What happens first? Begin the sequence on the board. Extend the activity by asking children to write a chart of their whole bedtime routine. Write each event under the previous one and draw an arrow in between.
● Check the sequence and explain that we can use similar charts to show sequences like a food chain or the water cycle.
● Cover the title of the photocopiable sheet and ask the children to read the text quickly and suggest what it shows. Ask them to identify where the process described begins and recap how the arrows show us in which order to read the sentences.

Shared sentence- and word-level work
● Ask questions about the chart such as:

> What is the first thing that happens on the chart?
> What is the second thing?
> What is the sixth thing?

● Write first, second, third, fourth, fifth, sixth, seventh, eighth, ninth, tenth, eleventh and twelfth on the board and relate them to numbers in a list.
● Most children will be able to give the date of their birthdays (*second, nineteenth, twenty-fifth*). Show them that by learning these words they will be able to write their birthdays in words as well as in numbers. Talk about the way in which we use abbreviations when giving dates in numbers and words (*2nd, 3rd, 4th, 21st...*).

Guided and independent work
● Support a group as they complete their lists and answer the questions. Discuss spellings with them and guide them as they write.
● Show them examples of other flow charts and cycles in books and, if possible, on websites and discuss how they are set out.
● Ask the children to complete the lists they were writing in the previous lesson before going on to answer the questions on photocopiable page 127.

Plenary
● Ask children to help you to complete photocopiable page 127. Display the flow chart prominently next to it.
● Revise the spellings and uses of *first, second, 12th* and so on.
● Ask those children who wrote additional questions to help you to write these on the board, and ask other members of the class to help you to answer them in complete sentences.

Differentiation

Less able
● Provide children with more partially completed sentence answers. For example, *Which is the last item in the flow chart?* could become *The last item on the chart is ___.*

More able
● Encourage children to find other flow charts in books and on websites.

Birthday present

Shared text-level work

● Recall the flow chart for organising a birthday party. Ask the children to help you to create a similar flow chart for giving a birthday present.
I   Begin by asking them to talk with partners about everything that is involved in giving a birthday present. List their suggestions on the board. Have some ideas ready, such as:

● *Get some money from the bank;*
● *Go to the shops;*
● *Choose a suitable gift;*
● *Take it to the checkout;*
● *Pay for it;*
● *Take it home.*

● The statements are written in the style of instructions, with each beginning with an imperative verb. Discuss how to turn them into explanations. For example: *First, you need to get some money from the bank so that you will be able to buy the present. Next, you go to the shops to look for presents.*
● When the class is happy with the list, give out strips of paper and ask small groups to write one point on their sheet in large letters, allocating these so that the more able write more challenging sentences.
● Attach all the sheets to the board, then ask the children to place them in an appropriate order. Use the words *first, second, third, then, next* and so on. Arrange the sheets in order one beneath the other and draw an arrow between them.

Shared sentence-level work

● Ask the children if they can suggest other ways in which the pieces of paper could be arranged. For example, they could be arranged across the board with horizontal arrows linking them; or they could be arranged as a series of steps:

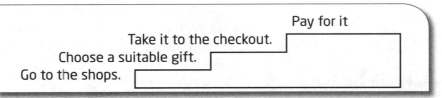

Guided and independent work

● Ask the children to draw a chart either for organising a birthday party or for giving a present. Encourage them to plan their charts and the number of items they will include before they begin setting them out.

Plenary

● Share the children's charts with the whole class and compare different layouts. Have they all included the same points?
● Write the beginnings of the months of the year on the left-hand side of the board and ask the children to complete the spellings.

My birthday party

A few weeks ago, my mum asked me if I would like a party to celebrate my seventh birthday. I said, "Wow, yes please Mum!" and she smiled and said, "I thought you'd be pleased! But if we are going to have a party, we will all have to work hard to get ready for it. Let's start by making a list of all the things we need to do."

So Mum, Dad and I sat at the table and made a list. We crossed some things out and added some others, and by the time we had finished and Dad had copied the list out neatly it looked like this:

Having a party seemed to be hard work, but we shared the jobs out, and even my little brother helped by tidying his toys away. We had the party yesterday and it was brilliant. Now we have made another list – of all the things we need to do to clean the house up after all the mess my friends made!

1. Decide where to hold the party.
2. Make a list of people to invite.
3. Write out invitations.
4. Send out invitations.
5. Buy food for the party.
6. Make a birthday cake.
7. Decorate the cake.
8. Tidy the house.
9. Make a list of games to play.
10. Buy prizes for games.
11. Prepare food for the party.
12. Have the party!

How a birthday party is planned

Decide where to hold the party.

⬇

Make a list of people to invite.

⬇

Write out invitations.

⬇

Send out invitations.

⬇

Buy food for the party.

⬇

Make a birthday cake.

⬇

Decorate the cake.

⬇

Tidy the house.

⬇

Make a list of games to play.

⬇

Buy prizes for games.

⬇

Prepare food for the party.

⬇

Have the party!

The birthday party flow chart

1. The third item in the flow chart is _____

2. The sixth item in the flow chart is _____

3. Which is the last item in the flow chart?

_____

4. Which of these would you do first: write invitations or

send out invitations? _____

5. Which of these would you do first: decorate the cake

or make the birthday cake? _____

6. What is the ninth item in the flow chart?

_____

7. What is the tenth item in the flow

chart? _____

8. What is the eleventh item in the flow

chart? _____

▪ Now make up two questions about the
chart for a friend to answer.

UNIT 1

Narrative 1

This unit is based around two famous traditional stories written by the brothers Grimm and comprises ten days' literacy activities supporting the NLS medium-term plan focus on different stories by the same authors. The children will explore plot, character and setting and story language. The unit also makes use of a brief biography of the Grimms, and leads up to extended independent story writing. This unit also covers *Developing early writing*, unit D and *Progression in phonics*, step 7.

Hour	Shared text-level work	Shared word-/ sentence-level work	Guided work	Independent work	Plenary
1 The brothers Grimm	Reading a biography of the brothers.	Learning new words and using them in context.	Re-reading the biography and asking questions.	Writing questions for each other.	Holding a quiz about the brothers.
2 The Elves and the Shoemaker – part 1	Reading of part 1 of a story, using context to help with new words.	Reading dialogue with appropriate expression and intonation. Empathising with character.	Writing new dialogue and preparing it for performance.	Adding dialogue then devising short dramatic presentations.	Performing dramatic presentations for the class.
3 The Elves and the Shoemaker – part 2	Speculating on rest of story before reading.	Rewriting story sentences in the past tense.	Oral retelling of middle part of story orally.	Writing own versions of the middle part of the story.	Reading stories aloud and comparing with original.
4 Writing an ending	Re-reading middle part of story before writing ideas for an ending, focusing on story language	Writing further sentences, constructing carefully and punctuating properly.	Continuing writing from previous lesson; discussing and writing a story ending.	Continuing writing from previous lesson; discussing and writing a story ending.	Reading aloud and noting good sentences and story language.
5 Stating preferences	Reading part 3 and comparing with the children's versions.	Using cards to identify and understand new words.	Compiling a chart to compare original and retellings, using ICT.	Discussing opinions and compiling comparison chart.	Presenting views and revising new words.

UNIT 1

Hour	Shared text level work	Shared word/ sentence level work	Guided work	Independent work	Plenary
6 The Musicians of Bremen – part 1	Reading the first part of another story, using context to help with new words.	Using punctuation to read aloud expressively.	Practising reading dialogue with tone and expression.	Practising reading dialogue with tone and expression.	Performing to the class. Using new words in sentences.
7 The Musicians of Bremen – part 2	Reading part 2. Speculating on the ending.	Looking at the suffix *-ful*.	Discussing ideas for ending the story.	Writing an ending for the story.	Sharing story endings. Looking at words with the suffix *-ful*.
8 The Musicians of Bremen – part 3	Shared reading of part 3, adding missing words.	Reading, sounding and spelling new words from the text.	Exploring how best to read dialogue.	Exploring how best to read dialogue.	Performing dialogue for the class. Evaluating performances.
9 Comparing stories	Discussing elements of the two stories.	Writing about views on the two stories.	Chaired discussion of story preferences.	Discussing and writing about story preferences.	Sharing views and choosing favourites.
10 Extended story writing	Writing opening for own traditional tale.	Revise words in Appendix List 1.	Producing collaborative story.	Extended writing of story.	Discussing progress of stories so far.

Key assessment opportunities
● Do the children understand concepts of authorship and publication?
● Do they read expressively?
● Can they evaluate stories and express preferences?
● Can they write stories, using complete sentences?
● Have they learned unfamiliar words?

UNIT 1 HOUR 1 ▭ Narrative 1

The brothers Grimm

Objectives

NLS
T2: To use phonological, contextual, grammatical and graphic knowledge to work out, predict and check the meanings of unfamiliar words and to make sense of what they read.
T5: To read about authors eg other books written, whether author is alive or dead; to become aware of authorship and publication.
W9: To learn new words from reading linked to particular topics.

What you need
● Photocopiable page 140.

Shared text-level work
● Explain to the children that they will be learning about two brothers who collected stories that people used to tell to their children, but which had not previously been written down. They will first find out about the Grimm brothers, and then read two of their best-known stories.
● Ask the children to look at photocopiable page 140 briefly. Ask them what the title is and what information they think the text includes.
● Read the text together, and then ask some comprehension questions about it. For example:

● Where were Jacob and Wilhelm born?
● Which brother was the elder?
● How many brothers and sisters did they have?
● What did they study at university?
● What were they interested in?
● Encourage the children to look at the text with partners to find the answers and write simple answers on whiteboards or paper.

Shared word-level work
● Write some of the less familiar words on the board, such as *Germany, difference, childhood, secondary, nearby, Law, librarian, interest, collected* and *enjoyment*.
● Involve the children in establishing the meanings and spellings. Then say some incomplete sentences and ask the children to choose the most appropriate word to complete each one. For example:

● _____ is a country.
● After primary school, children go to _____ school.
● The _____ in age between Jacob and Wilhelm Grimm was one year.

Guided and independent work
● Work with a lower ability group to support their reading. Help them to understand the biographical style and the content, and encourage them to use their existing skills to read difficult words and phrases.
● Encourage them to ask you and each other questions about the text.
● Provide each pair of children with photocopiable page 140. Ask them to read it together and then make up their own questions for classmates to answer. Provide small pieces of paper with sufficient room for the question and an answer.

Differentiation

Less able
● Ensure that each table has at least one good reader who can advise others.

More able
● Ask children to look at selected websites to find out more about Jacob and Wilhelm Grimm. (You could try www.pitt.edu/~dash/grimm.html, for example.)

Plenary
● Ask each pair to sit with another pair and exchange questions. Ask the children to read each other's questions and answer them.
● After a few minutes, ask some children to share their questions with the class and discuss the answers.
● Finally, use some unanswered questions to hold an informal quiz to see how much the children have learned about the Grimm brothers.

Objectives

NLS
T9: Through shared and guided writing to apply phonological, graphic knowledge and sight vocabulary to spell words accurately.
S1: To read text aloud with intonation and expression appropriate to the grammar and punctuation.

S&L
24 Drama: To present parts of traditional stories, own stories for members of the class.

What you need
● Photocopiable page 141.

The Elves and the Shoemaker – part 1

Shared text-level work
● Explain to the children that in this lesson they will be reading the first part of one of the Grimm brothers' most famous stories.
● Read the story opening. Pause at the words *business, surprise* and *beautiful* and ask the children to put up their hands if they know the words, but not to say what they are just yet.
● Remind the children that we can work out what a word might be by reading to the end of a sentence and then using the context, together with initial sounds, to predict what the word might be and what it might mean.
● Re-read the text with the children.

Shared sentence-level work
● Now look again at the middle paragraph in which the shoemaker speaks sadly about his lot. Read his speech, and then ask the children to read the lines aloud to a partner.
● Talk about the importance of looking carefully at punctuation and vocabulary to help us to read text with appropriate expression. For example, there is a comma for a slight pause, and two exclamation marks, and we are told that the shoemaker spoke *sadly*.
● Ask at least two children to 'play' the shoemaker and to say his lines aloud for the rest of the class.
● Read the final paragraph to the children again and ask them to think about what the shoemaker might have said when he discovered that the shoes had already been made when he came down the next morning.
● Write their ideas on the board and ask them to say the lines with appropriate expression and intonation.

Guided and independent work
● Work with a middle-ability group to guide their writing and discuss how they might say their lines for maximum dramatic effect.
● Ask the children to work in pairs to read part 1 of the story and to plan short dramatic presentations of the story so far.
● Explain that they may think of lines for the shoemaker's wife to say and that all of the story so far must be presented as far as possible through speech.
● Encourage them to write down lines and to practise saying them in preparation for performing them in the plenary.

Plenary
● Ask some of the pairs to perform their lines.
● Praise them for using expression and intonation to make their presentations lively and interesting.
● Explain that in the next lesson they will be reading the middle part of the story.

Differentiation

Less able
● Ensure that weaker readers are paired with more able readers so that they can participate fully, even if they encounter problems in reading the text.

More able
● Encourage children to look at examples of speech in texts and to model their punctuation on these.

The Elves and the Shoemaker – part 2

Objectives

NLS
T10: To write sustained stories, using their knowledge of story elements: narrative, settings, characterisation, dialogue and the language of story.
S3: To use standard forms of verbs in speaking and writing and to use the past tense consistently for narration.

What you need
● Photocopiable page 142.

Shared text- and sentence-level work
● Ask the children to remind each other of the story so far, then give you the sequence of events. Write these on the board.
● See if anyone knows the whole story already. If any children do, organise them into pairs to discuss the next section, while other pairs discuss what they *think* might happen next.
● Read the second part of the story, then compare the printed version with the children's ideas.
● Explain that this version of the story was written by a modern author and that there are many different versions. Remind the children that Jacob and Wilhelm Grimm collected and wrote down stories that had previously only been told orally.
● Ask the children to think about how they would retell the middle part of the story and to discuss their ideas in pairs.
● Using the children's ideas, write two or three sentences on the board but leave the verbs in the present tense. For example:

> The shoemaker *leaves* the pieces of leather on his table every night.
> He *sells* the shoes every day.
> The shoemaker *buys* leather for more shoes.
> The elves *sit* on the table and *stitch* the shoes.
> The shoemaker's wife *makes* some clothes for the elves.

● Remind the children that in stories we usually write in the past tense, because we are describing events that have already happened.
● With the children's help, write the correct past-tense form of the verb in place of its present-tense form. Reinforce understanding by looking at further examples if necessary.

Guided and independent work
● Encourage children to discuss and then tell their own versions of the middle part of the story orally, before they begin writing it. Act as a scribe where necessary.
● Ask the children to write their own versions of the part of the story that they have just read and discussed. Remind them that they should write in the past tense, but encourage them to include dialogue, which may be in the present tense.

Plenary
● There will not be sufficient time for all children to read their stories to the class so allow time for them to read to partners before choosing some children to read to the class. Remind them of the importance of using appropriate intonation and expression when reading aloud.
● Compare the children's versions to the one on page 142.
● Pick out a few examples of past tense verbs and ask the children what the present-tense forms are.

Differentiation

Less able
● Children who are not in the guided group could work with more able partners to produce joint stories.
● Some children could use the word processor to write their stories.

More able
● Explain that in the next lesson they will go on to write the story ending, so they may begin to think of ideas for this if they finish their writing.

Writing an ending

Objectives

NLS
T10: To write sustained stories, using their knowledge of story elements: narrative, settings, characterisation, dialogue and the language of story.
S5: To write in clear sentences using capital letters and full stops accurately.

What you need
● Photocopiable page 142
● the children's work from Hour 3.

Shared text-level work
● Discuss the events in the story so far and ask the children to think about how the story might end. Encourage them to share their ideas with a partner and to make brief notes on paper or whiteboards.
● Re-read photocopiable page 142 to the children as they follow and then ask them to suggest an opening line for the final section.
● Model writing the sentence for the children and encourage them to look at it critically and suggest ways in which it might be improved. For example, they might wish to change the word order, add adjectives or adverbs or change a verb to a more powerful alternative.
● In order to focus on the type of language used in stories, occasionally make a 'mistake' when writing so that children think carefully about the features of narrative. For example, you might write a verb in the present tense when the past tense would be more appropriate, or you could repeatedly write *said* in dialogue before asking for alternatives such as *cried, shouted* or *whispered*.

Shared sentence-level work
● With the children's help, write further sentences for the story ending, editing and revising and reminding the children about the use of capital letters and full stops.

Guided and independent work
● Ask the children to continue their writing from the previous lesson and go on to write an ending for the story. Once again, make some deliberate errors to encourage them to correct you and to explain what you have done wrong.
● Discuss the features of narrative with the children and encourage them to make use of dialogue.
● Encourage them to discuss their ideas as they write; share their thoughts and show their partners what they have written so far. Suggest they use these opportunities to check spellings and punctuation, but to make intelligent 'guesses' at spellings at other times, before checking them later. Remind them about using context to predict the meanings of words.

Differentiation

Less able
● Encourage children to check spellings *after* they have been writing, so their flow of ideas is less interrupted.

More able
● Let children word-process their stories and introduce pictures from illustration packages.

Plenary
● Choose some children to read their story endings to the class, reminding them about the importance of using appropriate intonation and expression.
● Write some examples of interesting sentences on the board and discuss these in terms of typical story language. If appropriate, invite the class to suggest alternative phrasing and vocabulary for the authors to consider.
● Discuss the use of capital letters and full stops and encourage the children to help you place them in the sentences.
● Explain that in the next lesson the children will have the opportunity to compare the published story ending with their own versions.

Stating preferences

Shared text-level work
● Read the story ending and ask the children for their opinions of it. Do they like the ending? Do they wish the elves had not disappeared? Was the shoemaker's wife right to give them gifts?
● Were the children's endings different? Which do they prefer? Why?

Shared word-level work
● Give out the cards with the words *elf-sized, woollen, jacket, tiptoed, downstairs, figures, chimney, scramble, table-top, delight, sewed, shiny, preferred* and *workshop* on them. As you do so, ask the class to say the words and ask the children who receive them to say them.
● Ask the children with word cards to come to the front and to hold their cards in front of them. Talk about the meanings of each word and, where appropriate, about different forms of the words. For example, *prefer*, which was written on the board at the beginning of the lesson, becomes *preferring* in the story and could also be *preferred*.
● Ask questions such as *Which person is holding the word 'scramble'?* and *Who has the word that means made of wool? Whose word means something you would find on the top of a house?* Continue until you feel that the children have understood the words.
● Re-read the story ending. Ask the children to look out for the words they are holding and to hold up their cards when they hear their words.

Guided and independent work
● Explain that you would like the children to look at their own story endings and at the published version to decide which they prefer and why. Ask them to make notes on the things they like and dislike about each and justify their opinions. Ask them to make a table like this:

The published ending	My story ending
Like it because the elves get a reward for their hard work	Like it because the elves come and live with the shoemaker and his wife.
Don't like the ending because the elves disappear	Don't like the way the shoemaker becomes lazy

● Work with a group using ICT. Hold a group discussion, then ask the children to produce their charts on a word processor.
● Remind them to justify, discuss and record their views on each point.

Plenary
● Discuss the opinions and ask the children if they would have written their retellings differently if they had seen the published ending.
● Finally, hold up the word cards one at a time and challenge the children to read them aloud and explain what they mean or use them in a sentence.

The Musicians of Bremen – part 1

Objectives

NLS
T2: To use phonological, contextual, grammatical and graphic knowledge to work out, predict and check the meanings of unfamiliar words and to make sense of what they read.
S1: To read text aloud with intonation and expression appropriate to the grammar and punctuation.

S&L
24 Drama: To present parts of traditional stories for members of their class.

What you need
● Photocopiable page 144.

Shared text-level work
● Explain to the children that they will be reading another story from the collection of Jacob and Wilhelm Grimm.
● Show them the story and ask them to read the title. Ask what musicians do. Explain that Bremen is a real town in Germany, although the story is fiction.
● Begin reading the first two paragraphs to the children.
● For the second paragraph, pause at the word *strolling*, pretend not to know the word and then read to the end of the sentence. Ask the children who already know the word not to say what it is and ask the others to think what the word might be. Read the opening clause again, replacing *strolling* with *mmm*, and ask the children if they can tell what *kind* of word it is. Can those who already know the word suggest words that do not begin with *s* but which would fit the context, such as *walking, ambling, marching* or *trotting*?
● Talk about the importance of working out what a word is and defining it using the letter sounds and context.
● Continue to read the story, pausing at *continued* in the same paragraph and asking the children to work out what the word might be.
● Finish the text, and then read it again with the children, asking confident readers to read the animals' dialogue.

Shared sentence-level work
● Focus on the dialogue. Talk about the different punctuation marks that help the reader to know how to read the lines. Ask other able readers to read the parts of the farmer, donkey, dog and cat.
● Encourage other children to try the lines, and then discuss different ways in which they may be said so that those listening understand when a question is being asked, a statement made or someone is surprised, excited, angry and so on.

Guided and independent work
● Ask the children to work in groups of four to practise reading the lines in preparation for performance. Allocate parts, and ask them to concentrate on the dialogue, using the speech marks to guide them as to which words should be spoken.
● Help them to develop appropriate intonation and expression when reading, but encourage them not to exaggerate gestures, levels and tones and to consider the listeners' enjoyment.

Differentiation

Less able
● Children may find it helpful to have the speech highlighted for them in different colours for the different parts.

More able
● Ask children to write additional dialogue for the animals and add this to their performance.

Plenary
● Ask some of the groups to present their interpretations of the dialogue.
● Look at the words *strolled* and *continued* and challenge the children to think of sentences that could include them. Encourage the children to use dialogue to replace narrative where appropriate.

Objectives

NLS
T1: To reinforce and apply their word-level skills through shared and guided reading.
T9: Through shared and guided writing to apply phonological, graphic knowledge and sight vocabulary to spell words accurately.
W7: To spell words with common suffixes, eg *-ful*.

What you need
● Photocopiable page 145
● dictionaries and thesauruses.

Differentiation

Less able
● Ask children what words they would like to include and then list some of those that they may need but find difficult to spell.

More able
● Let children use dictionaries or thesauruses to find other appropriate *-ful* words.

The Musicians of Bremen – part 2

Shared text-level work
● Recall the events in the story so far. Write key words on the board, including the characters' names.
● Read the second part of the story, with some children taking the parts of the donkey, cat, dog and cockerel.
● Now talk about the final sentence and ask if it makes them want to know what happens next. Discuss *cliffhangers* and the way in which they are used to encourage people to follow the next episode of a story.
● Ask the children to suggest what might happen next. Write some of their ideas on the board and discuss them.
● Explain less familiar words in the text, such as *cockerel, complain, concert, travelling, announced* and *unfortunately*.

Shared word-level work
● Draw attention to the word *wonderful* in the dog's first speech. Ask the children if they can think of other sentences that might include the word. Write some of these on the board.
● See if the children can think of other words that end with *-ful*. If necessary prompt them by suggesting *beautiful, delightful, hopeful, helpful, useful*.
● Talk about the 'root' words and how *-ful* is usually added to change a word from a noun (often abstract: *beauty, delight, hope, help, use*) into an adjective. Demonstrate that such words have a single *l* at the end.
● Produce further adjectives ending with *-ful* from *truth, care, colour, peace, thank, pain* and *cheer*.
● Brainstorm other words that end with *-ful*. (If they suggest skilful, you will need to explain that skill loses an l when the suffix is added.)

Guided and independent work
● Work with a group to brainstorm and discuss ideas before writing the next part of the story. Encourage children to tell you *why* they think the story will continue in a particular way and to refer to the story so far.
● Ask the children to work in pairs to write an ending for the story. Let them draw on photocopiable page 145 for ideas and help with spellings.
● Encourage the children to make use of words with *-ful* endings in their writing where appropriate.

Plenary
● Ask the pairs to read their stories to each other and to the whole class in some cases.
● Discuss their ideas. Talk about happy and sad endings and the tradition of having good triumph over bad in folk tales like this. Can they think of any more examples of stories in which good triumphs over evil? Why are traditional and fairy stories like this?
● Pick out examples of adjectives with *-ful* endings that the children have included, and ask the class for the noun forms.

Objectives

NLS
T1: To reinforce and apply their word-level skills through shared and guided reading.
S1: To read text aloud with intonation and expression appropriate to the grammar and punctuation.
W1: To secure phonemic spellings from previous 5 terms.

S&L
13 Speaking: To speak with clarity and use intonation when reading and reciting texts

What you need
● Photocopiable page 146.

The Musicians of Bremen – part 3

Shared text-level work

● Ask the children to think about the endings they wrote in the previous lesson and explain that they will read the ending from the published version and decide which they prefer.
● Before reading the text cover the following words:

Paragraph 1 – *shouted, night* and all but the suffix *-ful* in *beautiful.*
Paragraph 3 – *imagined*, except for the *i.*
Paragraph 5 – all *sleeping* and *horrible*, except the *s* and *h.*
Final paragraph – *victory*, except for the *v.*

● Start reading the story and explain that you will say *Mmm* whenever you come to a word that is fully or partially covered and that you would like the children to think about what the words might be, without saying them out loud.
● Having read the story once, ask the children to discuss the missing words in the first paragraph in pairs and to write on their whiteboards or paper what they think they are.
● Read the first paragraph with the children and ask them to include their suggested missing words. Stop and discuss the children's suggestions. Praise children who suggest words that would fit but differ from those in the published text. For example, *yelled* or *cried* instead of *shouted, evening* for *night, wonderful* for *beautiful.*
● Continue for the other paragraphs.
● Ask the children for their views on the story ending and compare it with their own versions.

Shared word-level work

● Look at some other difficult words in the text and discuss strategies for spelling them. For example, *frightened* has *fright* at the beginning, which has the same cluster of letters as *night, right, bright* and so on; *surprised* has an *r* before the *p, supper* has two *p*s so it is pronounced differently from *super*, which only has one.

Guided and independent work

● When most children feel confident about the vocabulary in the story ask them to work in threes with two as the robbers and one the narrator, to practise reading the text aloud.
● Encourage them to experiment with different ways of reading the story until they feel happy that they could read the text aloud to classmates successfully.

Plenary

● Ask some groups of children to read the text for the rest of the class.
● Invite comments about the expression and intonation used and gather suggestions for different ways in which the text might be read.

Differentiation

Less able
● Less able readers could play the parts of the robbers, as they have fewer lines.

More able
● Encourage children to add further dialogue to make the story more interesting.

Comparing stories

Objectives

NLS
T4: To compare books by same author: settings, characters, themes; to evaluate and form preferences, giving reasons.
S5: To write in clear sentences using capital letters and full stops accurately.

S&L
15 Group discussion and interaction: To listen to each other's views and preferences.

What you need
● Photocopiable pages 141–146.

Shared text-level work
● Explain to the children that they are going to discuss and compare the two Grimm tales and discuss which they liked better..
● Produce a chart like this one on the board:

Story feature	The Elves and the Shoemaker	The Musicians of Bremen	My preference with reasons
Settings			
Characters			
Themes			
Events			

● First, ask the children to decide what the settings are for each story. If necessary, explain that the setting includes *when* as well as *where* the story took place. Allow a few minutes for discussing this in their groups before sharing ideas as a whole class.
● Ask the children to look at the opening lines of each story and to compare these with their suggestions. 'The Elves and the Shoemaker' begins with *Once, long ago, in a small town…*, while 'The Musicians of Bremen' begins *Many years ago, in a tiny village in Germany.*
● For 'The Elves and the Shoemaker', the children might add *in a house*, and *on a farm* and *in the countryside* for 'The Musicians of Bremen'.
● Now talk about and list the characters in the stories.
● Go on to discuss the story themes. In the first story this might be that one good turn deserves another, while in the second there is a strong theme of friendship as well as of good triumphing over bad.

Shared sentence-level work
● Encourage the children to offer their opinions as to which of the stories they prefer and why. Note these in the chart.
● Ask the class to help you to write these in complete sentences.

Guided and independent work
● Work with a group to develop their discussions about the stories.
● Act as a chairperson to manage the discussion, and take notes on some of the things the children say so that they can reflect on these and decide if their views have been changed through discussion.
● Ask the children to identify and discuss settings, characters and themes. Ask them to refer to the chart and to write sentences about the two stories, stating which they prefer and why, which characters they like best and which setting and them they prefer.

Differentiation

Less able
● Support children with more able partners or classroom assistants.

More able
● Ask children to read other stories by the Grimm brothers and expand their charts to include them.

Plenary
● Ask the children to discuss their choices with partners, and then choose some to share them with the whole class.
● See which story is preferred by the majority of children before and after the discussion.
● Ensure that everyone understands setting and characters.

Extended story writing

Objectives

NLS
T10: To write sustained stories, using their knowledge of story elements: narrative, settings, characterisation, dialogue and the language of story.
W4: To secure reading and spelling of all the high frequency words in Appendix List 1.
W8: To spell common irregular words from Appendix List 1.

What you need
● Photocopiable pages 141 and 144
● NLS Appendix List 1
● dictionaries.

Differentiation

Less able
● Produce a shared story made up by the children but largely written down by you with occasional contributions from the children.

More able
● Some children may wish to write their own story openings rather than using the one from shared work. Ensure children understand that they should introduce the setting and some characters.

Shared text-level work
● This lesson should afford the children time to begin a story and develop it. Allow additional time for them to complete the story.
● Begin by discussing some of the things the children have learned during the unit. Talk about and write on the board *setting, character, theme, sentence, dialogue, author, past tense* and so on.
● Explain to the children that you would like them to help you to plan a story and write a story opening that gives the setting and makes the reader want to find out what happens next.
● Recall how traditional tales often begin, referring to the Grimms' stories as appropriate. Then ask for suggestions for a setting for the story and an opening line. Encourage the children to discuss stories they know and consider typical openings. Consider who might feature in the story and some of the events that might happen.
● Write the sentence on the board. Then read it and ask how it might be improved. Revise the sentence until you are all happy with it, and then ask for a suggestion for the next sentence. Ensure that some of the characters are introduced in these sentences.
● Carry on until there are three or four sentences of which you approve on the board.
● Explain that this is the opening of their story, and that they will introduce other characters and decide what happens in the remainder of the story. They must all keep to the same story opening, but they can develop the remainder of the story however they choose.

Shared word-level work
● Read through the words in Appendix List 1 with the children. Note any that they do not understand or cannot read and talk through them.
● Display the words prominently so that everyone can see them and use them to check spellings when writing their stories.

Guided and independent work
● Work with a group of lower ability children, but include some very able children, to discuss a story and then produce it collaboratively. Involve the more able children in writing ideas down and in writing on the board with your guidance.
● Ask the children to continue the story that was started on the board, working individually or in pairs. Advise them that they will be able to finish it in a later session. Remind them to read and revise at regular intervals what they have written, in order to improve the sense and expressiveness of the story.

Plenary
● Share some of the children's stories so far. Do they all continue in a similar way?
● Ask children to comment constructively on each other's work. Discuss how well the stories fit with the story opening and predict what might happen next.

The brothers Grimm

Jacob and Wilhelm Grimm were two brothers born more than two hundred years ago in Germany. There was only one year's age difference between them, so they were always close friends as well as brothers. When Jacob was born in 1785 there was already one older boy in the family, and after Wilhelm came seven more younger children. The family was not rich, and the two boys shared a bed in their childhood.

Jacob and Wilhelm were only 10 and 11 when their father died, and when the time came for them to go to secondary school, they left home to live with an aunt in a nearby town.

They both did well at school, and went on to university to study law. However, what they were really most interested in was finding out about the hundreds of old stories that older people in the country used to tell to children. In 1806 the two young men started to travel around the country, getting country folk to tell these stories, and then writing them down so that others could study them.

In 1808, their mother also died, and Jacob and Wilhelm had to leave university and take jobs as librarians to earn some money. They kept up their interest in the stories, and in 1812 they brought out a book containing 86 folk tales and fairy tales. Two years later, a second book retold 70 more such stories. Tales such as 'Rapunzel', 'Rumpelstiltskin', and 'Hansel and Gretel', which had been told by parents to their children for years, were first collected and written down by Jacob and Wilhelm Grimm. If they had not done this, all these stories might have been forgotten long ago!

The brothers lived to be old men, and never lost their enjoyment of the old stories. A great German university gave them special awards to thank them for all the work they had done for children.

The Elves and the Shoemaker – part 1

Once, long ago, in a small town, there lived a shoemaker. His business was not going well and he was very poor. Each day when he sold some shoes, he would use some of the money to buy leather so that he could make more pairs to sell on the following day. At last, a day came when he could only afford enough leather to make one more pair. That evening, the shoemaker cut out the shapes for the new shoes, and left the pieces of leather on his table as he went to bed.

"Oh dear!" he said sadly to his wife. "Tomorrow it will take me most of the day to stitch those shoes together, and then I must sell them quickly or we shall not be able to buy any food for our dinner!"

The next morning, when he came downstairs, the shoemaker had a huge surprise. In the middle of the table, where he had left the leather pieces, he found a beautiful pair of shoes already made. The stitches were so fine and tiny, and the decoration sewn so neatly on the toes, that he was able to sell the shoes straight away and for a much higher price than usual. That day he had enough money to buy leather for two more pairs.

The Elves and the Shoemaker – part 2

The next night, the shoemaker again cut out the pieces before he went to bed, and again he left them on the table in his workshop. The following morning, he found that both pairs had been carefully stitched together during the night. Again, he was able to sell the fine shoes for a very good price!

For a week, this went on. Every day the shoemaker was able to buy enough leather for more and more pairs of shoes, but no matter how many pairs he cut out, he always found them perfectly made up the next morning. At last, he decided to find out how this work was being done.

In the middle of the night, when all was dark and silent in the house, the shoemaker tiptoed downstairs and peeped through the crack of the workshop door.

Sitting cross-legged on the table were two little elves, bare-skinned and bright –eyed, stitching away to shape the flat pieces of leather into the finest shoes. Because the elves were so small, their stitches were also tiny, so now the shoemaker understood why the work was so very neat and fine. He tiptoed back upstairs and went back to bed.

In the morning, he told his wife what he had seen. "We owe our new good fortune to these kind elves," he said.

"We should find some way to thank them," said his wife.

"Elves are strange creatures," replied the shoemaker. "They like to do things in secret. They might not be happy if they knew I had seen them."

"Still," insisted his wife, "they have helped change our lives around. They deserve a reward. You said they had no clothes; it must be very cold for them sitting in your workshop in the middle of the night! Winter is coming, so I shall make them some warm clothes to wear."

The Elves and the Shoemaker – part 3

The shoemaker's wife fetched her workbox and spent the day sewing two elf-sized sets of clothes, with warm red woollen jackets and hats, bright blue trousers, checked shirts, and even tiny socks to keep their toes warm.

That night, when the shoemaker and his wife went to bed, they left these clothes laid out on the work-table with all the leather for tomorrow's shoes. When midnight came, the shoemaker tiptoed downstairs again to see what would happen.

He saw the two little brown figures slip down the chimney and scramble up the chair and onto the table. When they reached the table-top, the elves saw the clothes and held them up with little shouts of delight. They dressed themselves and were so pleased with their gifts that they danced round and round the table, before sitting down to do their night's work. They sewed quickly and neatly, and the next morning there were twenty pairs of shiny new shoes on the table for the shoemaker to sell.

"You see!" said his wife. "I told you they would be pleased with such a present!"

But the shoemaker was right about the elves preferring to keep their lives a secret. Now that they knew they had been seen, they never visited the shoemaker's workshop again.

The Musicians of Bremen – part 1

Many years ago, in a tiny village in Germany, there was a donkey who lived on a farm. He had worked hard for many years, pulling the farmer's cart and giving the children rides on his back. At last the farmer said to him, "You deserve a happy retirement, old friend. It's time to do what you want with your own life."

The donkey was very pleased. He thought about what he would like to do and decided that he would like to be a famous singer. Everyone had always admired his loud braying. "The whole world will want to come and hear me sing," he thought. "I'd better move to a large town with a good concert hall. Bremen is a big place – I'll go there." So he set off for Bremen.

As he was strolling along the road, his head full of plans for his new life, he was interrupted by a loud bark. Looking down, he found that he had trodden on the paw of a dog lying by the side of the road. "I'm awfully sorry!" said the donkey. "I didn't see you there. I hope I haven't hurt your paw."

"No, not at all," said the dog. "Where are you off to?"

"Oh, I'm off to Bremen to become a famous singer. Why don't you come with me? That's a nice loud bark you have!"

"All right," agreed the dog, and the two new friends continued along the road.

Soon they passed a little stone house. A large ginger cat was lying on the wall, and she waved her tail to the friends.

"Good morning!" said the donkey.

"Good morning to you," said the cat. "Where are you two going? It's not every day one meets a donkey with a dog."

"We're going to Bremen," said the dog.

"What are you going there for?"

"We're going to be famous singers," explained the donkey.

"I can sing too," said the cat. "Everyone listens when I sing at night. Some people call it yowling, but I prefer to call it singing."

"Why don't you come to Bremen with us, and we shall all sing together?" asked the donkey.

"I should love to!" replied the cat, and she jumped onto the donkey's back so that they could carry on along the road.

The Musicians of Bremen – part 2

The next animal they met was a cockerel, who was standing beside the road crying "Cock-a-doodle-doo!" over and over again at the top of his voice.

"My dear sir," said the dog, "has anyone ever told you that you have a wonderful voice?"

"No," said the cockerel. "People more often complain when I start to sing, and shout that they want to sleep."

"Come to Bremen with us, and join our group of concert musicians!" suggested the cat.

"Thank you, I'd love to,"

So now there were four friends travelling to Bremen. Before long it started to get dark, and the group decided that they should find a place to spend the night. They saw a little house in a field, and thought this looked a good place to stay.

"There is a field of nice green grass for me to munch," said the donkey.

"There is a smoking chimney, so there must be a warm fire for me to curl up by," said the cat.

"There is a ball in the yard for me to play with," said the dog.

"There are beams for me to sit on and practise my singing," said the cockerel, "but maybe someone already lives here?"

"We shall sing to them, and they will be so pleased that they will let us stay the night!" announced the donkey happily.

So the four friends all began to sing their very loudest, outside the windows of the house. Unfortunately, they all sang different songs at the same time, so the sound they made was a kind of, "MEEOW MEEOW WOOF WOOF HEE-HAW HEE-HAW COCK-A-DOODLE-DOO!"

The Musicians of Bremen – part 3

The robbers were very frightened by the tremendous noise right outside the house. "It must be ghosts!" shouted one. "Quick, let's run away!" And the two men ran out of the house as fast as they could.

The animals were surprised to see two people run away so quickly, instead of thanking them for the beautiful concert, but they realised that now the house was empty they would all be able to sleep there anyway. They moved in, and after enjoying a good supper, they all settled down for the night in comfort.

The robbers, meanwhile, were feeling rather silly at having run away so fast. "There couldn't really have been a ghost," said the first one. "That noise must have been something else."

"Perhaps we just imagined it!" said his friend. "Let's go back to the house."

The first robber quietly pushed open the door.

The dog was sleeping just behind the door. He woke up to find a strange foot on him, and he bit the leg hard. When the robber cried out, the other animals woke.

At once the man found himself attacked by claws, paws, hooves, a beak, furry and feathery wings and legs and tails. The noise of the animals was even louder than the song they had sung outside the window.

The frightened robber escaped as quickly as he could, and this time the two men kept going all night and didn't even think

about going back to that horrible haunted house!

As for the musicians, they sang a song to celebrate their victory, and agreed to share their home for the rest of their days.

So they all settled down happily together – but, strange to tell, they never did become famous musicians.

UNIT 2

Non-fiction 1

This unit is based around common wild flowers of the UK and comprises five days' literacy activities to support the medium-term plan focus on information texts. The activities will help children to develop their ability to read and understand different types of texts and to use texts as a starting point for posing questions and producing their own non-fiction texts. The unit can be linked to Science 2: *Find out about the different kinds of plants and animals in the local environment.* Ideally, this unit is best done in June when the flowers mentioned should be in bloom. Unit 2 also covers *Developing early* writing, unit G and unit I, and *Progression in phonics*, step 6 and step 7.

Hour	Shared text-level work	Shared word-/ sentence-level work	Guided work	Independent work	Plenary
1 Buttercups, daisies and dandelions	Asking questions about plants in school grounds. Reading about wild flowers.	Learning new words and compound words and using them in sentences	Sounding and spelling new words, using similarities with known words.	Writing sentences to include new words.	Sharing and developing sentences.
2 Nettles, speedwell and thistles	Reading about other wild flowers. Discussing differences between fiction and non-fiction.	Turning statements into questions	Re-read the text and note layout features.	Writing questions for classmates to answer using the text and other sources.	Answering the questions as a class.
3 Recording information	Scanning text for information. Using charts/tables.	Entering information in chart, using commas to separate items in lists.	Completing the chart and looking for more information to include.	Discussing information and completing the chart.	Compiling a class chart.
4 More common wild flowers	Reading about more wild flowers.	Looking at new vocabulary in context. Writing sentences and checking punctuation.	Adding further information to wild flower charts in note form.	Adding further information to wild flower charts in note form.	Completing the class chart and creating a display.
5 Making a wild flower booklet	Reviewing information gained about wild flowers.	Developing information from the chart into sentences.	Producing pages for a class information booklet.	Producing pages for a class information booklet.	Compiling the booklet.

Key assessment opportunities
● Can the children distinguish between fiction and non-fiction and identify layout features?
● Do they write in complete sentences?
● Can they write questions?
● Can they scan texts to answer questions?
● Have they learned new topic words and how to spell them?

Objectives

NLS
T18: To evaluate the usefulness of a text for its purpose.
S5: To write in clear sentences using capital letters and full stops accurately.
W9: To learn new words from reading linked to particular topics.

What you need
● Photocopiable page 153
● pictures of wild flowers, or the real thing from the school grounds (as long as they aren't rare species).

Buttercups, daisies and dandelions

Shared text-level work
● Encourage the children to look for (but not pick) wild flowers during playtime and at home.
● Show the children the wild flowers or pictures and ask see if they can identify any. Leave them on display and write these questions on the board: *Are there daisies in our school grounds? Are there dandelions?*
● Ask the children to read the questions and to offer answers. They may have noticed the flowers and be able to say where they have seen them. Write some of their answers on the board in sentences.
● Ask the children to ask other questions about daisies and dandelions.
● Read the first three entries on photocopiable page 153. Ask what kind of text it is and what its function is.
● Ask the children if the descriptions help them to identify the flowers. Look at pictures and ask if anything further could be added to the descriptions which would make it easier to identify flowers.
● Ask for outstanding questions now that they have read the text.

Shared word- and sentence-level work
● List some of the less familiar words in the text, such as *common, grounds, stain, meadows, verges, pastures, leafless, petals, especially, whereabouts, roadsides, wasteland, woodland.* Explain their meanings and help the children to spell some of them.
● Talk about the compound words *whereabouts, roadsides, wasteland, woodland.* See if the children can split them into their component parts.
● Look again at the full list of unfamiliar words and work with the children to write sentences to include them. Talk about capital letters, full stops and parts of speech.
● Read and redraft as necessary. Encourage the children to be critical of the sentences and suggest possible changes.

Guided and independent work
● Work on the sounds and spellings of the listed words again and think about other words that have similar features, for example *sound/ ground, stain/rain, meadow/head, petal/pedal, whereabouts/where, wasteland/taste.*
● Ask the children to write their own sentences that include the words listed on the board. Their sentences don't need to be about flowers, they can be about anything.

Plenary
● Ask the children to share their sentences, initially with a partner from a different table, and then share some with the class.
● Write examples on the board, check everyone's understanding and ask how the sentences could be made more interesting. For example, sentences could be combined using connectives, or additional information could be added.

Differentiation

Less able
● Provide more able partners for struggling readers and/or writers.

More able
● Challenge children to write sentences for all of the words on the list, including some that contain more than one of the words.

ALL NEW 100 LITERACY HOURS · YEAR 2

Nettles, speedwell and thistles

Objectives

NLS
T13: To understand the distinction between fact and fiction.
T14: To pose questions and record these in writing, prior to reading non-fiction to find answers.
T17: To skim-read title, illustrations and subheadings, to speculate what a text might be about.
S6: To turn statements into questions, learning a range of *wh* words typically used to open questions: *what, where, when, who* and to add question marks.

What you need

● Photocopiable page 153
● examples and/or pictures of wild flowers
● books and/or CD-ROMs of wild flowers
● high frequency words on card.

Differentiation

Less able
● Help children to read each sentence and then stop to consider what question it would answer before reading on, to keep the chunks of information small.

More able
● Give access to additional resources. Ask children to make up further questions for each other.

Shared text-level work

● Show the children rest of photocopiable page AA. See how quickly they can tell you the names of the wild flowers described. Do they notice anything about the way the text is organised? How are the definitions ordered? (Alphabetically.) What is the purpose of the subheadings? Can the children tell what the text is about without having to read it all? Does the text tell a story or is it non-fiction? (It is non-narrative, alphabetical, has subheadings and so on.)
● Read the descriptions of nettles, speedwell and thistles.
● Discuss what the children have found out about all of the flowers. Write questions about each while they look at the text to find answers.
● When they offer answers, ask for them in complete sentences. Encourage children to tell you how they found out the answer.

Shared word- and sentence-level work

● Go through any unfamiliar words.
● Focus on the description of nettles. Ask the children to think of questions that someone reading the text might want to know and could find out by reading the text. For example, *What colour are nettles? Can they sting? Do all varieties sting? Where are they found?* Ask other children to point to the answers.
● On separate cards, write the following words: *buttercups are yellow*, and a full stop. Ask three children to hold a word each and another to hold the full stop, and get them to arrange themselves in the right order to form a sentence. Note that *buttercups* should have a capital letter as it begins the sentence.
● Now write a question mark card and ask a child to replace the full stop. Ask the children to rearrange themselves so that the sentence becomes a question. Which word should have a capital letter now?
● Discuss other ways in which a question could be asked about the colour of buttercups (*What colour are buttercups?*). Using some of the sentences from the photocopiable page write questions using *which, why, where* and *what*.

Guided and independent work

● Re-read the text. Discuss the layout and show how to use headings and subheadings to find information.
● Organise the children to work in pairs to re-read the whole text and produce questions for their classmates.

Plenary

● Ask volunteers to put their questions to the class. Write some examples on the board, leaving out the initial *wh* word and closing question mark for the children to add. Then challenge the children to use the text to answer the questions. Write the answers under the questions in complete sentences.

Recording information

Shared text-level work
● Re-read photocopiable page 153. Recap the information it provides and the features of its layout.
● Explain that the same information, or much of it, could be presented in different ways. Demonstrate how a chart presents information concisely so that readers may locate quickly the information they are seeking. Show the children photocopiable page 155 and ask the children to tell you what kind of information should go in each cell. For example, the second column has the heading *colour(s)*, so that is the column where we should write the colour of each flower. Demonstrate how to read across the rows and down the columns.
● Talk about strategies for locating text through scanning. Look carefully at the word you want to find; think about which section of the chart it might be in; scan down the column or across the row to see if you can find it.
● The third column can also be completed using the information text. The fourth can be used later when children find flowers in the school grounds. For the final column, the children may wish to add other information they have found.
● Emphasise that when writing information in charts we usually just write relevant key words such as *yellow*, or *meadows, fields, grass verges and pastures*.

Shared sentence-level work
● Because many of the sections in the chart will require children to provide more than one item in a list, they will need to separate the words or phrases by using commas (as in the last example above).
● Highlight examples in the text. Try reading them without the commas to reinforce why they are needed, and then model transferring the information to the chart.

Guided and independent work
● Work with a higher ability group to complete the chart and scan other sources (including the internet if possible) to add other wild flowers to the chart and to present information about them.
● Ask the children to complete as much of the chart as possible by working in pairs or small groups to scan photocopiable page 153. You may wish to divide the task up so that in a group of six each pair completes information for two flowers.

Plenary
● Use the information the children have gleaned to complete a chart for the whole class. If the guided group added to the chart, include their information too.
● Ask the children to advise you on how to present the information in the chart. Where are commas needed?
● Talk about the different ways in which this information could have been represented.

More common wild flowers

Shared text-level work

● Show the children photocopiable page 154. Explain that this text gives more information about other wild flowers. See if the children can tell you which flowers are described here. They should be able to do this quickly by using the subheadings, but help them with unusual names such as *campion* and *sorrel*.
● Read the text with the children. Then pick out colour words and ask which flower is which colour. Show any examples you have in the classroom.
● Remind the children how they can present information like this more concisely by using the chart on photocopiable page 155.

Shared word-level work

● Look at some of the new words, such as *purplish, pinkish, supposed, diamond, papery, soldiers, battlefield, during, appear, daylight, opposite* and *vinegar*. Talk about the sound–symbol correspondence that helps us to pronounce them. Do they know any words that could help them interpret what the unfamiliar words mean? Ask: *What does purplish sound like? Why has the writer said* purplish *instead of purple.*
● Help the children to understand the unfamiliar words by re-reading them in context, then writing some of them in other sentences with their help. If they find it difficult to work out the meaning by context, allow them to look the definitions up in dictionaries.
● As you read what you have written, encourage the children to check on where you have placed capital letters and punctuation, including commas in any lists.

Guided and independent work

● Ask the children to work in pairs or small groups to add information from photocopiable page 154 to their charts. Again, you may wish to divide the flowers between members of the group so that each pair focuses on two.
● Spend time establishing/revising the meanings of new vocabulary in the text.
● Remind children how to find the key pieces of information in each section and the best ways of reducing this for presentation in the charts.

Plenary

● Ask the children to read from their charts to help you to complete the class chart.
● Talk about ways of presenting information concisely and about the importance of using commas to separate items in lists. Talk about the different ways of presenting information, for example, tables, charts, flow charts and so on.
● Display the class wild flower chart prominently and add photographs of the relevant wild flowers. Ask children to help you to make labels for the flower images.

Making a wild flower booklet

Objectives

NLS
T20: To write non-fiction texts, using texts read as models for own writing, eg use of headings, subheadings, captions.
S5: To write in clear sentences using capital letters and full stops accurately.

What you need
● Photocopiable pages 153–155
● good quality paper for writing and drawing
● examples of wild flowers
● resources on wild flowers
● a blank class booklet with at least 16 pages.

Differentiation

Less able
● Support children to word-process their text, encouraging them to use the spell checker.

More able
● Encourage children to research other common wild flowers. You may want to include foxglove, oxe-eye daisy, vetch and bird's-foot-trefoil.
● Children could go on to make a contents page, once the text is completed.

Shared text- and sentence-level work
● In this final lesson, the children draw upon their knowledge of non-fiction texts to produce a class booklet about common wild flowers. The time spent on whole-class work should be reduced, giving additional time for group work. In order for the children to produce illustrations to accompany their writing, you may wish to provide additional time after the lesson.
● Begin by reviewing the work done and by looking at the class wild flower chart. Pose questions about the information on the chart, such as *What colour are buttercups? Where might you find bluebells? Which flower is sold each November?*
● When children answer the questions encourage them to respond in complete sentences, and write these on the board, taking prompts from the children.

Guided and independent work
● Explain to the children that they are going to produce their own booklet about common wild flowers so that children in other classes and in next year's Year 2 may find out about them. Stress that they will need to present their work very neatly and carefully.
● Consider how the information could be presented. Talk about the use of separate sections with subheadings, and labelled illustrations. Explain that the text should be presented in complete sentences, like those on photocopiable pages 153 and 154.
● Give each pair of children the task of writing about one wild flower from photocopiable page 153 or 154, using all the information they have gathered so far. Tell them to share and discuss information first, and then to write their paragraph in their own words. Remind them to start it with a subheading.
● Encourage children to try out their sentences orally before attempting to write them, and guide them towards accurate spelling by referring them to the texts provided.
● Those who finish their work during the lesson should go on to write about other common wild flowers or make a start on illustrating their flower.

Plenary
● Ask the children to bring their writing to the plenary. Discuss layout and spellings and praise the quality of each piece of work.
● Ask them to help you to arrange the sheets in alphabetical order so that they can be placed in the booklet. Remind children that if necessary, we can use second and third letters and so on to put words into alphabetical order.
● You may wish to stick the sheets into the booklet straight away, but you could leave this for a few days so that some children have the opportunity to add text on other wild flowers.
● If possible, take children to a local park or green area to see real examples of wild flowers.

Common wild flowers

Depending upon the whereabouts of your school, you will find different wild flowers growing in the grounds. Here are some of the most common wild flowers.

Buttercup
Buttercups have golden yellow flowers. They can be found on the banks of rivers and ponds, in weedy places in gardens, and in wet fields and meadows. Buttercups grow best in damp places.

Daisy
Daisies turn towards the sun. The flowers close up at night and in wet weather. They can be found in meadows, fields, grass verges and pastures. Each flower has a leafless stalk. The flowers have a yellow centre and white petals. Sometimes the petals are partly pink as well as white.

Dandelion
Dandelions can be found almost anywhere, but especially in fields, gardens, meadows, roadsides and on wasteland. The flowers are yellow and the stems are leafless with white sap inside. The sap can leave a brown stain on the skin when handled.

Nettle
Nettles are very common on land that has been disturbed. They can often be found in places where buildings once stood. The flowers can be white, pink or yellow. Some nettles sting if you touch the leaves.

Speedwell
Speedwell are blue. They grow in fields, wasteland, woodland, and weedy places in gardens.

Thistle
There are many different types of thistle. Thistles are very common on grassland. Most varieties have purple flowers and prickly leaves, but some have yellow flowers.

More common wild flowers

Bluebell

Sometimes a carpet of bluebells covers the ground in a wood or forest. The flowers are shaped like bells and are most often purplish blue or blue, although sometimes they are pink or white. They flower from April to June.

Clover

Clover flowers are usually white or purplish red. Clover can be found on grassland and it flowers from May to September. Clover is eaten by cattle. The leaves are green with white marks. There are usually three leaves to each stem. Finding a four-leaved clover is supposed to be lucky.

Fat hen

Fat hen can usually be found in farmland and on wasteland. It is often one of the first wild flowers that appears on bare soil. The leaves can be oval or diamond-shaped. It has spikes of white flowers that appear from June to October.

Poppy

Poppies grow on farmland and wasteland. The red poppy flower has four papery petals and it appears from June to August. Every November paper poppies are sold to raise money for soldiers who were injured in battle. The poppy is used because it was the first thing to grow on battlefields after fighting had ended.

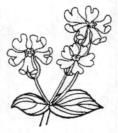

Red campion

There are many types of campion. Red campion has pairs of hairy leaves that grow from opposite sides of the stem. The pinkish-red flowers, which appear during daylight, have five petals and appear from March to October. Campions grow in wet areas.

Sorrel

Sorrell can be found in all sorts of grassy places. It has deep green, arrow-shaped leaves that taste of vinegar and are often used in salads. Red flowers appear from May to July.

Wild flower chart

◾ Use the descriptions of wild flowers to complete this chart.

◾ Add other wild flowers you find out about.

Wild flower	Colour(s)	Where found	Where found at school	Interesting features
Daisy				
Dandelion				
Buttercup				
Nettle				
Speedwell				
Thistle				

UNIT 3

Poetry

This unit is based around language play and, in particular, alliterative tongue-twisters in poetry. The activities will help children to revise their existing phonic knowledge and develop it further and enable the children to become more comfortable with blends and digraphs studied in previous terms. This unit also covers *Developing early writing*, unit 14 and *Progression in phonics*, step 5.

Hour	Shared text-level work	Shared word-/ sentence-level work	Guided work	Independent work	Plenary
1 Big black bug bites big black bear	Reading a tongue-twister based around **b** and **bl** sounds.	Finding further words beginning with **b** and **bl** and writing them in simple tongue-twisters.	Writing tongue-twister sentences.	Using dictionaries to help in writing tongue-twisters.	Trying to say the tongue-twisters!
2 Cooking cookies	Reading of a tongue-twister with **c** words.	Identifying parts of speech. Looking at hard and soft c in common words.	Classifying **c** words by sound and finding others.	Sorting words into hard and soft **c** and **ch**.	Creating class lists of **c** words.
3 Selling seashells on the seashore	Reading a tongue-twister with **s** and **sh** words.	Brainstorming **s** and **sh** words for a tongue-twister.	Writing a tongue-twister. Practising dictionary skills.	Writing tongue-twisters and practising saying them.	Trying out the tongue-twisters.
4 Weathering the weather	Reading a tongue-twister with **w** and **wh** words. Distinguishing meanings of **whether** and **weather**.	Exploring spellings of **wh** and **w** words and writing alliterative lines.	Using dictionaries to build up lists of **wh** and **w** words before writing simple poems.	Using dictionaries to build up lists of **wh** and **w** words before writing simple poems.	Sharing and adding to poems.
5 Writing tongue-twisters	Re-reading tongue-twisters. Writing alliterative lines based on the children's names.	Looking at names with irregular spelling patterns.	Writing name-based tongue-twisters, using dictionaries to find suitable vocabulary.	Writing name-based tongue-twisters, using dictionaries to find suitable vocabulary.	Sharing children's tongue-twisters and discussing spellings.

Key assessment opportunities
● Do the children understand that the same sound can be made by different letters?
● Can they read, say and write tongue-twisters?
● Can they spell words using phonemic spellings learned previously?

Big black bug bites big black bear

Objectives

NLS

T1: To reinforce and apply their word-level skills through shared and guided reading.
T11: To write tongue-twisters.
W1: To secure phonemic spellings from previous 5 terms.

What you need
● Photocopiable page 162

Differentiation

Less able
● Children may need to work with more able pupils who have found several *bl* words that they can use in their sentences.

More able
● Ask children to make up short verses with a preponderance of *bl* and *b* words.
● They could go on to use other onsets to create tongue-twisters.

Shared text-level work
● For this first lesson, a sentence that includes several words beginning with *b* or *bl* has been chosen. There are no alternative spellings for these initial sounds, and this allows the children to focus on the nature of an alliterative tongue-twister without the complications of spellings.
● Read the first tongue-twister on photocopiable page 162 to the children, and then ask them to have a go at reading it to themselves, slowly at first, but then increasingly quickly.
● Explain that tongue-twisters are generally designed to be difficult to say, so that people make mistakes that are funny and can sometimes be rather rude!
● Ask the children if they know of any other tongue-twisters and to share them with the class. Write some examples on the board and have fun trying to say them.

Shared word-level work
● Look closely at the first tongue-twister again and talk about the beginnings of the words (the onsets). Most of the words begin with either *b* or the consonant blend *bl*.
● Ask the children if they can tell you other words that start the same as *black, bleed* and *blood* and write these on the board.
● Provide simple dictionaries for some children to look up and share words that begin with *bl*.
● With the children's help, write a simple tongue-twister in which most words begin with *bl* or *b*. This should take the form of a simple sentence.

Guided and independent work
● Guide a group with their attempts to write tongue-twisters, helping them with spellings and discussing their choices of vocabulary in terms of sentence construction.
● Ask children to use simple dictionaries to find as many recognisable words as they can that begin with *bl*. Ask them to include as many as they can in their own tongue-twister. Point out that not every word has to begin with *b* or *bl*, but that the tongue-twister will be more effective if they do.

Plenary
● Ask the children to share their tongue-twisters firstly with their neighbours and then with the whole class.
● Have fun saying them together. Challenge children to say them as quickly as they can.
● Discuss the words they have chosen and write some of the less familiar ones on the board so that you can introduce or reinforce spellings. Praise imaginative vocabulary.

Cooking cookies

Objectives

NLS
T9: Through shared and guided writing to apply phonological, graphic knowledge and sight vocabulary to spell words accurately.
S2: To understand the need for grammatical agreement, matching verbs to nouns.
W6: To investigate words which have the same spelling patterns but different sounds.

What you need
● Photocopiable pages 162 and 163

Shared text-level work
● Show the children the second tongue-twister and ask them to try reading it with their partners.
● Ask the children if it makes sense and if they understand it.

Shared sentence-level work
● Look at the word *cook* and explain that it can be a noun and a verb. Identify the different ways in which the word is used in the tongue-twister. In *How many cookies could a good cook cook?* it is first a noun, then a verb.
● Write some simple phrases on the board, such as *The cooks cook and the cook cooks*, and notice how the spelling of the verb changes to agree with the noun.
● Next, write simple questions, such as *What did the good cook cook?* Discuss the answer and write *The good cook cook cookies.* Ask if this sounds right, and then add an *-ed* past tense ending to correct it.

Shared word-level work
● Talk about the initial sound *c* as in *cook* and ask the children if this letter is always sounded hard, like a *k*. Can they think of any words in which an initial *c* is sounded differently? List a few from photocopiable page 163 in order to get them started.
● Then write various words that begin with *c*, and ask the children to decide whether they begin with a hard *c* or a soft *c*.
● Explain that words that begin with *c* and are followed by *i*, *e* or *y* almost always have a soft *c* (*city, cell, cycle*) while those followed by *a*, *o* or *u* tend to have a hard *c* (*cat, cod, cup*), as do those followed by consonants other than *h* (*clap, crack*).

Differentiation

Less able
● Provide struggling writers with the words cut out from photocopiable page 163 and, after discussion, help them to stick them into the columns.

More able
● Ask children to find and classify words that begin with or include a hard *c* sound but are spelled in different ways, such as *king, chemist, chicken, tikka, cobra*.

Guided and independent work
● Work with a group to guide their discussions about the *c* words and then ask them to look at other pieces of text and dictionaries to find more *c* words to classify. Write them in a table with the headings from photocopiable page 163.
● Provide photocopiable page 163 for each pair of children and ask them to sort the words into those that begin with a hard *c*, those that begin with a soft *c*, and those that begin with *ch*.

Plenary
● Ask the children to bring their word lists to the plenary and use them to create class lists.
● Remind the children about the work they did in Term 2 on words beginning with *ch* and ask if they can sort them by sound too (as in *church, chef, Christopher*).
● Say some words which begin with a k sound and ask the children if they can guess which letter each word begins with (try *kick, cup, cat, kitten, cage* and *king*). Point out that *ck* at the end of words such as *kick, brick*, and *lick* is a k sound.

Selling seashells on the seashore

Objectives

NLS
T8: To discuss meanings of words and phrases that create humour, and sound effects in poetry, eg tongue-twisters.
W1: To secure phonemic spellings from previous 5 terms.
W9: To learn new words from reading, to build collections of significant words.

What you need
● Photocopiable page 162
● dictionaries.

she	sells
shop	salt
shed	soap
shoe	say
sheep	said
shall	soup
shame	socks

Differentiation

Less able
● Encourage children to present their lists of s and sh words horizontally and in what they consider to be a logical order. Then help them to link the words into sentences.

More able
● Challenge children to write more complex tongue-twisters and to punctuate and spell accurately, using dictionaries.

Shared text- and word-level work
● Read the seashells tongue-twister to the children and then ask them to read it a few times.
● Ask them why it is so difficult to read. (The preponderance of similar-sounding words made up of *sh*, *s* and long *e* sounds makes it difficult to distinguish between the sounds in speaking.)
● Explain that you would like the children to help you to write a tongue-twister using *sh* and *s* words.
● First, brainstorm a list of words beginning with *sh* and another for those beginning with *s*, under the headings *she* and *sells*. For examples, see the table below.
● Create an additional column if anyone suggests words such as *sugar* and *sure,* which begin with *s* but have a *sh* sound.
● Ask the children to help you to write a tongue-twister that has a series of *sh* and *s* words. If they find it difficult to get started, suggest an opening such as these include:

> "Surely," said Sam, "someone should say something sensible about shopping for shoes in Sheffield."
> Seven sizzling sausages sat in Sîan's saucepan.

● As the children suggest words and phrases for the tongue-twisters, add any new words to the lists. Remind them to minimise the use of words that don't start with *sh* or *s*.

Guided and independent work
● Work with a group to support their tongue-twister writing.
● Spend time looking at spellings of *s* and *sh* words. Look at simple dictionaries with the children and discuss some of the words they find. Talk, too, about the layout of the dictionary and the information provided. What can we use dictionaries for? How do we know where to look for a particular piece of information?
● Ask the children to work in pairs to write tongue-twisters featuring words beginning with *sh* and *s*. Encourage them to use the list on the board for ideas, as well as a simple dictionary to find more words.
● When they have completed at least one tongue-twister, ask them to practise saying it so that they can share it with the class during the plenary session.

Plenary
● Share some of the tongue-twisters. Ask the children to say their lines slowly at first so that you can write them on the board, and then ask them to say them as quickly as they can without making mistakes.
● Challenge the rest of the class to try individuals' tongue-twisters. Which are the most difficult?
● Add any new words to the lists created in shared work.

UNIT 3 HOUR 4 ▸ Poetry

Weathering the weather

Shared text-level work

● This lesson should provide an opportunity to revise work from Term 2 on the digraph *wh*, as well as enabling children to write more extensive tongue-twisters.

● Show the children the rhyme about the weather and read it to and then with them.

● Practise reading it a couple of times, taking note of the punctuation and rhythm.

● Pick out the words *whether* and *weather*, write them on the board, and discuss their different meanings. Check that the children have understood, by saying sentences that contain them and asking the children to point to the version used. For example:

> ● I love sunny weather.
> ● He couldn't decide whether to buy an ice cream or not.
> ● I don't know whether to go to Hull or not. It depends on the weather.

Encourage the children to make up sentences of their own too.

Shared word-level work

● In some versions of this rhyme there is an additional line before the last one: *Whatever the weather*. Tell the children about this and ask them to help you to write the line on the board, asking them to tell you which version of *weather/whether* is needed, and establishing the spelling of the compound word *whatever*.

● Read the rhyme again quickly, inserting the additional line.

● Work with the children to write alliterative statements about the weather. Ask them to suggest appropriate words beginning with *wh* or *w*, for example, *windy, wild, white, warm, wet, wind, whipping, whistling, whooshing*.

● Try out different alliterative sentences and then combine some to create a short poem.

Guided and independent work

● Ask children to use dictionaries to help them to find *w* and *wh* words in order to write simple alliterative poems about the weather. Suggest that they list the words alphabetically, using second and third letters to order them.

● Encourage them to work co-operatively in pairs or small groups to create joint lists from which all members of the group may draw. Remind them to only include words that they understand.

Plenary

● Share the children's alliterative lines and write them on the board.

● Invite other children to suggest additional words that could be used, and work together to write extra lines for some of the poems.

● Discuss the spellings of the additional words and write them on the board. Encourage children to sound the words in phonemes.

Writing tongue-twisters

Objectives

NLS
T11: To write tongue-twisters or alliterative sentences; select words with care, re-reading and listening to their effect.
W1: To secure phonemic spellings from previous 5 terms.

What you need
● Photocopiable page 162
● a list of the children's first names
● dictionaries

Shared text-level work

● Discuss the tongue-twisters read during the week's lessons. Ask the children which they liked best and why.
● Talk about some of the tongue-twisters the children produced themselves and re-read some of these.
● Ask the children to look at the list of their first names and to suggest at least one alliterative adjective for each. Invite the child whose name appears to make the first suggestion and then ask others for further ideas. Emphasise that the words don't necessarily need to be particularly suited to the person, but they should not suggest any adjectives that are unkind or negative about each other.
● Write out the words next to the child's name, so that a list is gradually created:

> Abigail – artistic
> Ben – bouncy, bright
> Chloe – clever.

● Now work together to write an alliterative line about one of the children. (To provide support for independent work, you may wish to choose a less able child who could then use the line as a starting point for his or her own writing.)
● Begin by writing at least one adjective, then the child's name, and add a verb and a noun. For example, *Bright, bouncy Ben baked buns.*
● Invite suggestions for further words to expand the sentence: *Bright, bouncy Ben baked blackcurrant buns brilliantly!*

Shared word-level work

● Ask the children to suggest suitable verbs and nouns for each other's alliterative sentences. Write some of these on the board and note any difficult spellings. For example, children with names such as Chloe, Charlotte, Sîan, Siobhan or Thomas will find that most alliterative words for their names begin with different graphemes from those that begin their names. Chloe will probably need to find words beginning with hard *c* or *k*, Sîan and Siobhan will need words beginning with *sh* or *ch* (as in *chef*), while Thomas will need words beginning with *t* (rather than *th*).

Guided and independent work

● Ask the children to use their dictionaries to find suitable words for their names and discuss some of their findings within their groups.
● Then ask the children to write simple alliterative lines about themselves. Encourage them to extend the lines and include adverbs where appropriate.

Plenary

● Have fun hearing the children's lines. Compare different lines for the same initial phoneme.
● Write some examples on the board and discuss spellings and especially the different ways in which some phonemes can be written.
● Ask children to add further words to the examples and discuss their spellings

Differentiation

Less able
● If possible, organise children to work with more able partners with the same initial sound to their name.

More able
● Encourage children to write at greater length and go on to write alliterative lines about famous people, friends or family.

Tongue-twisters

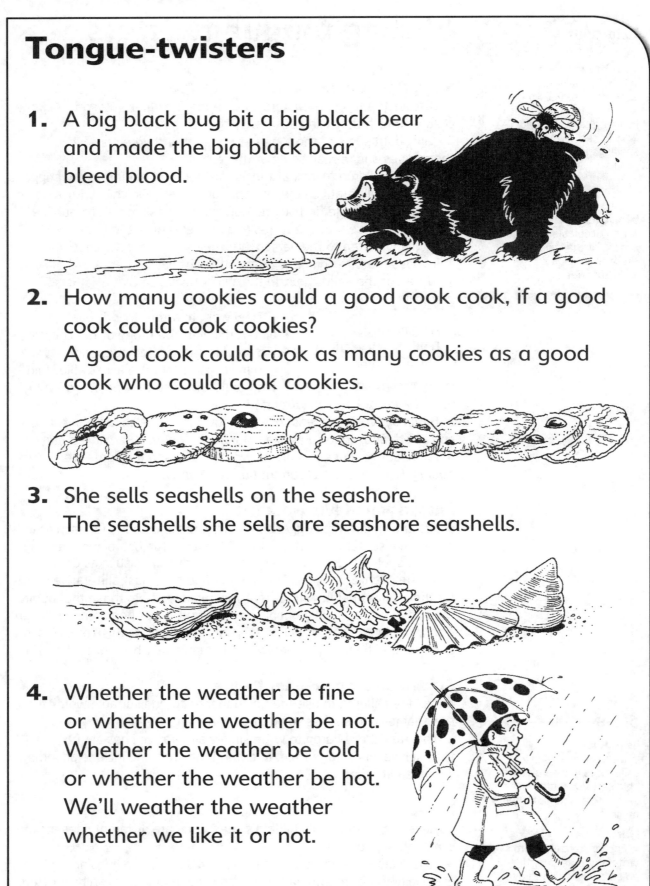

1. A big black bug bit a big black bear and made the big black bear bleed blood.

2. How many cookies could a good cook cook, if a good cook could cook cookies?
A good cook could cook as many cookies as a good cook who could cook cookies.

3. She sells seashells on the seashore.
The seashells she sells are seashore seashells.

4. Whether the weather be fine
or whether the weather be not.
Whether the weather be cold
or whether the weather be hot.
We'll weather the weather
whether we like it or not.

Hard or soft c?

◼ Read the words and sort them into those which begin with:
- hard c as in cat
- soft c as in city
- another, different sound.

cold	came	call	centimetre
can	circle	could	cycle
cinema	circus	carrot	cake
cut	cylinder	cinder	city
cow	card	colour	chip
chair	child	chef	Christmas
Chloe	Charlie	Charlotte	chew

ALL NEW 100 LITERACY HOURS · YEAR 2

UNIT 4

Narrative 2

This unit is based around *The Worst Witch* by Jill Murphy (published by Puffin) and will focus on extended stories by significant authors. The activities will help children to develop their appreciation of authorship and of the anatomy of a fiction book. It is important that the book is used as a class reader during the week. This will involve you reading parts of the story to the children at times outside the Literacy Hour.

Hour	Shared text-level work	Shared word-/ sentence-level work	Guided work	Independent work	Plenary
1 Introducing the Worst Witch	Looking at the book cover. Reading the story opening and meeting the characters.	Learning difficult words and compound words.	Re-reading the text and discussing the characters.	Completing statements about Maud and Mildred.	Sharing sentences and checking accuracy.
2 Jill Murphy	Reading and discussing an author biography.	Using new words in sentences to aid understanding.	Answering questions about the biography.	Answering questions about the biography.	Discussion about Jill Murphy's life and work.
3 Ethel the Pig	Further reading. Discussion of setting and characters. Reading dialogue aloud.	Exploring synonyms.	Listing synonyms. Practising dictionary skills.	Using dictionaries and thesauruses to replace synonyms in the text.	Suggesting synonyms for other words in the book.
4 The Broomstick Formation Team	Reading expressively. Predicting the ending.	Practising reading and spelling techniques. Revising synonyms.	Practising reading aloud. Noting any unfamiliar words.	Practising reading aloud. Noting any unfamiliar words.	Performing for the class. Reading the end of the story.
5 Evaluating the story	Discussing events, theme and characters, relating to other stories.	Identifying words useful in evaluating the book.	Group discussion of opinions and ideas about the book.	Writing simple evaluations of the story.	Sharing opinions and discussing evaluations.

Key assessment opportunities
● Do the children read expressively?
● Can they evaluate what they have read and give reasons for their opinions?
● Do they use context, grammar and phonological knowledge to predict meaning?
● Do they use synonyms in their writing where appropriate?

Introducing the Worst Witch

Objectives

NLS
T5: To read about authors from information on book covers, eg other books written, whether author is alive or dead, publisher; to become aware of authorship and publication.
W9: To learn new words from reading.

What you need
● *The Worst Witch* by Jill Murphy
● photocopiable page 171.

Shared text-level work
● Show *The Worst Witch* to the children and explain it is by a famous author. Ask them to find the title and the author's name.
● Look at the back cover and see who illustrated the book.
● Read the blurb and see if the children want to find out more.
● Ask how we could find out about the author. Show the biographical notes at the beginning of the book and explain to the children that they will be finding out more about Jill Murphy later in the week.
● Show a few illustrations to whet the children's appetite for reading the story. Then read the opening of the story. Explain that the main character is Mildred Hubble.
● Read photocopiable page 170 with the children. Ask them to describe Mildred and Maud. Write some of the descriptions on the board.
● Write sentence beginnings, and ask for suggestions as to how they might be completed. For example:

● Maud was…
● Mildred didn't mean to…
● Mildred often had her hat…
● Mildred's bootlaces…
● Maud wore…

● Comment on the children's suggestions, and explain that they will be completing them later.

Shared word-level work
● Pick out some of the difficult words, such as: *potion, laboratory, plaits, absent-mindedly, bootlaces, training* and *chewed*. Explain the meanings and, with the children's help, write sentences to include some of them.
● Look at *bootlaces* and note that two words are joined to make a compound word. Ask the children for other compound words. If necessary, prompt them by giving them words that often form the first part of a compound, such as *tooth(brush/paste), foot(ball/wear/stool/bath)*, and *some(one/thing/what/times)*.

Guided and independent work
● Work with one group to re-read the extract and then discuss the characters. Show the children how to scan the text to find information and refer to the text when making their points.
● Go back to the incomplete sentences about Mildred and Maud, and ask the children to find out information about the girls.
● Explain that they should not simply copy from the story, but think of different ways of phrasing where possible.

Differentiation

Less able
● Give children cloze sentences so they need only complete one or two words.

More able
● Encourage children to make up further sentences and to rephrase them so that they don't all begin with a child's name.

Plenary
● Share some ideas for completing the sentences. Write examples on the board. Ask the children to check their work as you do so.

UNIT 4 HOUR 2 ◼ Narrative 2

Jill Murphy

Objectives

NLS
T5: To read about authors from information provided.
W2: To reinforce work on discriminating syllables in reading and spelling.
W9: To learn new words from reading linked to particular topics, to build individual collections of personal interest or significant words.

What you need
● Photocopiable page 170
● a display of Jill Murphy's books
● access to selected websites about Jill Murphy (such as the author pages at www.penguin.co.uk)
● list or chart of questions about photocopiable page 170.

Differentiation

Less able
● Prompt children with key words to find and let them answer in note form rather than sentences.

More able
● Ask children to find more information on the internet and/or look at other Jill Murphy books see what biographical information has been added over the years.

Shared text-level work
● Ask the children what they can remember about Jill Murphy from the previous lesson. Show other books by her and explain, for example, that three of them are sequels to *The Worst Witch*, while some are written for very young children.
● Write the words *author* and *illustrator* on the board and ask the children what they think they mean.
● Read the short biography, discussing any words the children don't know. Encourage them to work out unfamiliar words by context, and to check definitions in the dictionary.
● Ask questions that can be answered by scanning the text. For example:

● How old was Jill Murphy when she wrote *The Worst Witch*?
● Who illustrates Jill Murphy's books?
● When did Jill Murphy give up her job to become a full-time author?
● What kind of pet does Jill Murphy have?
● Ask the children to look at the text and then discuss, in pairs, other questions they could ask. Share some of these with the class.

Shared word-level work
● Look at some of the less familiar words, for example *illustrator*, *stapler*, *published*, *various*, *concentrate*, *academy*, *popular* and *award*.
● Say each one in the sentence in which it appears in the text. Ask the children to discuss what the words might mean and to include them in sentences on their whiteboards or paper.
● Discuss the sentences with the children and address any misconception they may have about spellings and the meanings of the words.
● Now look at the word *concentrate*. Show how it can be broken up into syllables. Talk about the soft c that begins the second syllable and discuss other soft c words, such as *city* and *ceiling*. Remind the children that *c* is one of the letters that has more than one sound and ask them to look for the hard c in the same word.
● Encourage the children to break other words into syllables to help them to say and spell them.

Guided and independent work
● Provide each pair of children with a list of questions about photocopiable page 173, perhaps according to ability. In addition to those on the board, you could ask about when and where she was born, awards, family, other work and so on. Explain that they should look carefully at the biography to answer the questions.

Plenary
● Ask the children to bring their answers to the plenary.
● Answer the questions as a class, drawing upon the children's ideas.
● Share any additional information that children may have found.

Ethel the Pig

Objectives

NLS
T1: To reinforce and apply their word-level skills through shared and guided reading.
W10: To use synonyms and other alternative words/phrases that express same or similar meanings; to collect, discuss similarities and shades of meaning.

What you need
- Photocopiable page 172
- the Worst Witch
- dictionaries and thesauruses.

Differentiation

Less able
- Limit the number of words and restrict them to simpler words, such as *bad, funny* and *clever.*

More able
- Encourage children to look for synonyms for other words in the text, perhaps rewriting some sentences.

Shared text-level work
- Before this lesson you should have read pages up to the beginning of chapter 3 of *The Worst Witch*.
- Read the beginning of chapter 3 and talk about Ethel, and Mildred's relationship with her, and the setting of this chapter.
- Show the children the extract on photocopiable page 171 and read it to them. Re-read it with the children, asking one good reader to read Ethel's lines and another to read Mildred's lines. The rest of the class should read everything else aloud.
- Talk about what has happened in the story so far. Then ask the children what they think about how the story is written. For example, look at some of the words and phrases that help set the mood: *sneered, shriek of laughter, crowed, Cries and shouts rent the air, That's torn it!*
- Discuss the meanings of the words and phrases and how they inform our reading, and re-read the extract.

Shared word-level work
- Look at the words *bad, deliberately, miserable, clever, vanished* and *furious* and ask the children to discuss their meanings with partners.
- Begin with *bad* and ask for suggestions for synonyms. If children struggle to think of any, suggest contexts such as *a bad egg, bad weather* or *bad behaviour*. Ask them to think of other words which could replace *bad* in the phrases and write them on the board.
- Look at the other words in the same way and explain that we can improve our writing if we use synonyms to replace some instances of words that we tend to use a lot, such as *nice, good, big* and *small.*

Guided and independent work
- Work with a group to re-read the text and discuss synonyms and parts of speech. Go around the group to list as many syllables as possible for certain words.
- Revise dictionary and thesaurus skills.
- Ask the children to read the extract and find the following words: *bad, crashed, funny, clever, miserable, crowded, vanished, furious.*
- Ask them to re-read the sentences that include the words and to try to think of synonyms so that the sentences retain their meaning. Encourage them to use dictionaries and simple thesauruses.

Plenary
- Ask the children to discuss their sentences in pairs and as a class.
- Write some of the sentences on the board and address any misconceptions about word usage.
- Invite children to suggest synonyms for other words from the extract or earlier text in the book.
- Ask them to discuss synonyms in pairs and to play a game in which they take turns to say a synonym. For example, *big, large, enormous, gigantic*. Challenge children to see which pair can produce the longest string of synonyms.

The Broomstick Formation Team

Objectives

NLS
T2: To use phonological, contextual, grammatical and graphic knowledge to work out, predict and check the meanings of unfamiliar words and to make sense of what they read.
S1: To read text aloud with intonation and expression appropriate to the grammar and punctuation.

S&L
13 Speaking: To speak with clarity and use intonation when reading and reciting texts.

What you need
● Photocopiable page 173
● tape recorders.

Shared text-level work
● Before this lesson, you should have read and discussed the story up to the beginning of chapter 7.
● Explain the setting for this extract: a Hallowe'en celebration at which Mildred's class are performing a broomstick flying display for their teachers and the chief wizard.
● Read the extract to and then with the children, emphasising appropriate expression and intonation.
● Discuss the content and ask the children what they think will happen next. Tell them that you will read the end of the chapter (from the paragraph which begins *As soon as they had formed the circle*) at the end of the lesson.

Shared sentence-level work
● Look at some of the less familiar words to ensure that the children can read and understand them. For example: *frightening, piercing, arrived, embroidered, prepared, perfectly, received, applause, nose-dived* and *arranging.*
● Demonstrate how we can learn to spell some of these difficult words by focusing on the 'tricky' parts. For example, in *piercing* it is the *ie* that many people misspell, while in *received* it is the *ei.*
● Remind the children about synonyms and ask if they can suggest any suitable alternatives for some of these words. Write their suggestions on the board.
● Emphasise the importance of reading the whole sentence or paragraph when children meet an unfamiliar word as this can help them to understand what it might mean. Re-read a few of the sentences to reinforce this.

Guided and independent work
● Organise the children to work in small groups to read the extract and to practise performing it with appropriate expression and intonation. Encourage them to note in the margin of the photocopiable sheet any words or phrases that they don't understand, so that these can be discussed later.
● Encourage a more able group to discuss the story, organise themselves into different roles and perform the extract as a radio play. This could be recorded and played back during the plenary.

Differentiation

Less able
● Ensure children are able to work with better readers who can explain difficult words.

More able
● If possible, provide other groups with tape recorders. This will enable you to hear everyone's work, which might not be possible within the plenary.

Plenary
● Listen to the more able group perform the extract either 'live' or by playing the tape recording. Praise their use of expression and intonation and remind children that you will be looking for this when other groups perform.
● Ask others to perform the extract.
● Discuss any words or phrases that have presented problems.

Evaluating the story

Objectives

NLS
T7: To compare books by different authors on similar themes; to evaluate, giving reasons.
T12: To write simple evaluations of books read and discussed, giving reasons.
W9: To learn new words from reading linked to particular topics, to build individual collections of personal interest or significant words.

What you need
● A copy of *The Worst Witch* by Jill Murphy
● copies of other books by Jill Murphy.

Differentiation

Less able
● See Guided and independent work.

More able
● Encourage children to read other books about Mildred. Those who have already read these could write reviews for the series rather than just concentrating on *The Worst Witch*.

Shared text-level work
● Before the lesson, read the story up to the final chapter. Discuss the events and the role Mildred plays in saving her school.
● Re-read and discuss the final chapter.
● Prompted by the children, write the names of the main characters on the board. Ask the children which characters they liked and disliked and why. Write some sentences on the board to express some of the views.
● Where children say they don't like a character, ask them to cite an incident or incidents that influenced their opinions. Emphasise the importance of giving reasons for their views. How do we know that Mildred is a nice character despite not always doing the right thing?
● Talk about the setting and theme for the story and ask if the story or any parts of it remind them of any other stories. Many may suggest the Harry Potter stories by JK Rowling, also set in a school where children ride broomsticks and are trained in spells. Others may include Julia Donaldson's *Room on the Broom,* Valerie Thomas's *Winnie the Witch, The Jolly Witch* by Dick King Smith, *Pongwiffy* by Kaye Umansky and Helen Nicoll's *Meg and Mog* series. Also introduce the other books from the *Worst Witch* series, such as *The Worst Witch Strikes Again* and *A Bad Spell for the Worst Witch* (Penguin).

Shared word-level work
● Explain that the children are going to write personal evaluations of *The Worst Witch*. Ask the children to suggest some words they think they may need. Write these on the board for reference. Ensure that these appear in the list: *prefer, character, setting, opinion, view.*

Guided and independent work
● Ask children to write down their opinions, thoughts, feelings, impressions of *The Worst Witch*. Tell them to write in complete sentences about the characters they liked and disliked, about the setting, the illustrations, and what they liked or disliked about the story. Encourage them to refer to other stories they have read that have similar themes and to compare them with Jill Murphy's book.
● Work with a group of lower ability children to discuss the book and to try out their ideas orally before they begin writing them.

Plenary
● Ask the children to share their writing with partners and then with the class.
● Note any interesting or controversial opinions and write some example sentences on the board. Encourage the children to discuss each other's views on the book and to justify them by referring to the text. Ask them to discuss their views in pairs before sharing them with the class.
● If any children have also looked at other books in the series, ask them to talk about these. In particular, if they have enjoyed them, ask them to try to persuade others to read the books.

TERM 3

Jill Murphy

Jill Murphy is an author and illustrator. She was born in London in 1949, and from the age of six, she began writing and making books. She made her first books by joining the pages together with a stapler.

When she was 18, Jill wrote *The Worst Witch*, which was published in 1974. She worked at various jobs, including in a children's home and as a children's nanny, until she was 27, when she decided to give up her job and concentrate on being a writer and illustrator.

She has written four books about Mildred Hubble's schooldays at Miss Cackle's Academy for Witches. The stories have been made into a television serial which was very popular. Her other books include stories for very young children, such as *Peace at Last*. Her story *Five Minutes' Peace* won the *Parents* Best Books for Babies Award.

Jill Murphy lives in London with her son, Charlie, and her pet dog.

The Worst Witch: Extract 1

Mildred Hubble was in her first year at the school. She was one of those people who always seem to be in trouble. She didn't exactly mean to break rules and annoy the teachers, but things just seemed to *happen* whenever she was around. You could rely on Mildred to have her hat on back-to-front or her bootlaces trailing along the floor. She couldn't walk from one end of a corridor to the other without someone yelling at her, and nearly every night she was writing lines or being kept in (not that there was anywhere to go if you were allowed out). Anyway, she had lots of friends, even if they did keep their distance in the potion laboratory, and her best friend Maud stayed loyally by her through everything, however hair-raising. They made a funny pair, for Mildred was tall and thin with long plaits which she often chewed absent-mindedly (another thing she was told off about), while Maud was short and tubby, had round glasses and wore her hair in bunches.

Jill Murphy

Text and illustration © Jill Murphy

The Worst Witch: Extract 2

'I think Miss Cackle gave you that cat on purpose, Ethel sneered. 'You're both as bad as each other'.

'Oh, be quiet,' said Mildred, trying to keep her temper. 'Anyway, it's not a bad cat. It'll learn in time'.

'Like you did? Ethel went on. 'Wasn't it last week that you crashed into the dust-bins?

'*Look*, Ethel, Mildred said, 'you'd better be quiet, because if you don't I shall …'

'Well?'

'I shall have to turn you into a frog – and I don't want to do that,'

Ethel gave a shriek of laughter.

'That's really funny! She crowed. 'You don't even know the beginners' spells, let alone ones like that'.

Mildred blushed and looked very miserable.

'Go on, then!' cried Ethel. 'Go *on*, then, if you're so clever. *Turn* me into a frog! I'm waiting'.

It just so happened that Mildred did have an idea of that spell (she had been reading about it in the library). By now, everyone had crowded round, waiting to see what would happen, and Ethel was still jeering. It was unbearable.

Mildred muttered the spell under her breath – and Ethel vanished. In her place stood a small pink and grey pig.

Cries and shouts rent the air:

'Oh, no!'

'That's torn it!'

'You've done it now, Mildred!' Mildred was horrified. 'Oh, Ethel,' she said. 'I'm sorry, but you did ask for it.'

The pig looked furious.

'You *beast*, Mildred Hubble! It grunted. 'Change me back!'

At that moment Miss Hardbroom suddenly appeared in the middle of the yard.

Jill Murphy

The Worst Witch: Extract 2

'You may begin,' said Miss Hardbroom.

Ethel rose perfectly into the air, followed by the rest of the class. First, they made a line, sinking and rising, which received great applause. Then they nose-dived the yard. (Miss Cackle closed her eyes during this part, but nothing went wrong). Then the girls made a V in the air, which looked quite beautiful.

'Your girls get better every year,' remarked a young witch to Miss Hardbroom, who smiled.

Last of all came the circle, which was quite the easiest part.

'All over soon', whispered Maud, arranging her broomstick in front of Mildred.

As soon as they had formed the circle, Mildred knew that something was the matter with her broomstick. It started to rock about, and seemed to be trying to throw her off balance. 'Maud! She cried to her friend. 'There's something –' but before Mildred could say any more, the broomstick gave a violent kick like a bucking bronco and she fell off, grabbing at Maud as she fell.

There was chaos in the air. All the girls were screaming and clutching at each other, and soon there was a tangled mass of broomsticks and witches on the ground. The only girl who flew serenely back to each was Ethel. A few of the younger witches laughed, but most of them looked grim.

Jill Murphy

Text and illustration © Jill Murphy

UNIT 5

Non-fiction 2: Report

This unit is based on non-fiction texts about the experiences of Victorian children. It supports the NLS medium-term plan focus on non-chronological reports. You may wish to combine the activities with other work on Victorian times. The unit particularly links to history, RE and materials and their properties in science. There are many excellent websites available, such as www.learningcurve.gov.uk/victorianbritain/default.htm, www.channel4.com/learning/microsites/Q/qca/victorians/, http://telematics.ex.ac.uk/virvic/welcome.htm, to support study and research, and museums often have displays of Victoriana. This unit also covers *Developing early writing*, unit H.

Hour	Shared text-level work	Shared word-/ sentence-level work	Guided work	Independent work	Plenary
1 Victorian school life	Looking at pictures of Victorian school scenes and discussing before writing notes.	Developing simple sentences.	Making notes and then writing simple sentences describing school scenes.	Making notes and then writing simple sentences describing school scenes.	Presenting pictures and notes to the class.
2 A Victorian school room	Looking at pictures of Victorian school scenes and posing questions.	Writing questions using *wh* words.	Writing questions about Victorian lessons.	Writing questions about Victorian lessons.	Asking and attempting to answer the questions.
3 Teachers and lessons in Victorian times	Reading about Victorian schools to reviewing questions from previous lesson. Practising note-taking.	Looking at *r* and *wr* words. Learning new words related to Victorian schools.	Discussing the text. Practising scanning skills.	Making notes from text.	Using notes to precis text.
4 Slates, discipline and work	Reading more about Victorian childhood, making notes.	Learning new words. Developing notes into simple sentences.	Writing and linking complex sentences.	Writing simple sentences about the text.	Sharing sentences, noting use of commas in lists.
5 Facts about Victorian schools	Reading concise information about Victorian schools Discussion about facts and fiction.	Using synonyms to rewrite extracts from the text.	Rewriting information in own words.	Rewriting information in own words.	Comparing synonyms. Reinforcing concepts of fact and fiction.

UNIT 5

Hour	Shared text level work	Shared word/ sentence level work	Guided work	Independent work	Plenary
6 Writing under headings	Discussing features of non-fiction texts. Modelling writing under subheadings.	Writing correctly punctuated sentences.	Exploring various sources on the topic, comparing layout.	Extended writing about Victorian schools, using subheadings.	Talking about each other's work. Checking sentence punctuation and use of subheadings.
7 Questions about playing outside	Introducing text about Victorian games. Formulating questions.	Writing questions in complete sentences.	Writing questions about this and other texts.	Discussing and raising questions as a group.	Discussing how to find information in texts.
8 Playing outside in Victorian times	Using a text to answer questions. Highlighting key words.	Learning new words related to Victorian games.	Using notes to write about the topic in groups.	Using notes to write about the topic in groups.	Reporting to the class. Discussing layout features.
9 Sunday games	Reading about toys and games, making notes.	Learning new topic words and practising spellings.	Re-reading and using new words in sentences.	Using key words to answer questions.	Going over answers. Playing a game to revise new words.
10 Dolls and mechanical toys	Reading about toys and games in Victorian times. Asking questions about the text and noting answers.		Reading and making notes about dolls or mechanical toys.	Reading and making notes about dolls or mechanical toys.	Reporting about information found. Turning notes into sentences.

Key assessment opportunities
● Can the children distinguish between fact, fiction and non-fiction?
● Can they pose questions prior to reading to find answers?
● Can they make notes from non-fiction texts?
● Can they write non-fiction texts, using subheadings and correctly punctuated sentences?
● Have they learned new words?

Victorian school life

Objectives

NLS

T19: To make simple notes from non-fiction texts, eg key words and phrases, to use in subsequent writing.
S5: To write in clear sentences using capital letters and full stops accurately.

S&L

21 Speaking: To use language and gesture to support the use of diagrams when explaining.

What you need
● Photocopiable page 186.

Shared text-level work
● Introduce the pictures of Victorian school life and ask the children to study and discuss them with partners.
● Share their observations and note their comments on the board, for example *children sat in rows, the teacher had a stick, the class was very big*.
● Talk about making notes and show the children how to write very short phrases that briefly describe the pictures. These might comprise an adjective and a noun, for example *large class, big stick, high windows* or *wide age range*.
● Discuss any new words that children use and show the class how to spell these. List key words for the children to refer to when they are working independently.

Shared sentence-level work
● Take some of the statements the children have made and, with their help, write these in complete sentences, recalling the need to use capital letters and full stops.
● Use these to discuss the difference between notes and sentences, and explain to the children that they will be making notes about the pictures in preparation for writing in complete sentences.
● Talk about the appropriateness of each way of writing and how the style needed will depend upon the audience for whom it is written. For example, we often use note form when we are writing for ourselves because we are familiar with the information, but we use complete sentences when writing for others because we need to express new ideas clearly and the text needs to be nice to read. Explain that notes must be detailed enough that we can be able to understand what we meant when we come to share them with others.

Guided and independent work
● Organise groups so that each group focuses on a different picture at first. Ask the children to make notes about the picture in preparation for writing simple sentences. When the children have made notes on their allocated picture, they may go on to make notes on any of the others.
● Explain that each group will be asked to report back to the rest of the class on what they see in their pictures. If possible, give time for practising their presentation.
● When they have made their notes, they should write some of them in complete sentences.

Differentiation

Less able
● Ensure that children who might find note-making difficult can see the list of words on the board.
● Give children the same picture that you discussed in whole class work so that they have some ideas for their notes.

More able
Ask children to write more extensively, perhaps devoting a paragraph to each picture.

Plenary
● Ask each group to show its picture and to use the notes that they made to describe it and comment on it. Add any new key words to the list on the board.
● Look at some examples of complete sentences that children may have produced. Check punctuation and discuss again the difference between notes and sentences. Were the notes useful when speaking?

A Victorian school room

Objectives

NLS
T9: Through shared and guided writing, to apply phonological, graphic knowledge and sight vocabulary to spell words accurately.
T14: To pose questions and record these in writing, prior to reading non-fiction to find answers.
S6: To turn statements into questions, learning a range of 'wh' words typically used to open questions: *what, where, when, who* and to add question marks.

What you need
● Photocopiable pages 186 and 187
● pictures of Victorian school scenes.

Shared text-level work
● Look at the picture with the children and remind them about the notes they made in the previous lesson. With their help, make notes about this picture.
● Explain that you would like them to look more carefully at the picture and discuss with their partners anything they would like to know more about. For example, they may see a poster on the classroom wall in the picture or they may comment on what the children are wearing.
● Now ask the children to offer questions about the picture, and write some of these on the board.

Shared sentence-level work
● Write the words *when, why, where, what, who* down the left-hand side of the board. Notice the onsets and practise spelling the words. Ask the children to suggest sentences that could begin with the words. (Most of the suggestions will be questions.)
● Take some of the notes made in the previous lesson and some of the children's comments and questions from this one and write some questions based on them on the board. Encourage the children to begin these with *wh* words.
● Ask the children to discuss their ideas with partners before suggesting question sentences. If available, give each pair a mini whiteboard to try out their sentences and share them with the class.
● When writing the question sentences, occasionally 'forget' to include capital letters or question marks and encourage the children to spot and correct your mistakes.

Guided and independent work
● Ask the children to look at a picture of a Victorian school scene and to discuss it with their partners in preparation for writing questions about it. Explain that they will have the opportunity to find answers to their questions in subsequent lessons.
● Ideally, ask them to focus their questions on teachers and lessons. Ask them to look at the picture and pose question s such as *What is the teacher doing? Who is the person standing in the corner? Why does the teacher have a stick?*
● On the board, write a reminder to the children to check that their questions begin with capital letters and end with question marks.
● Support one group as they discuss their questions and write them. Talk about spellings of *wh* words, and emphasise the importance of using question marks.

Plenary
● Ask pairs to show their pictures and ask their questions. See if anyone can answer any of the questions.
● Explain that in the next lesson
the questions will be discussed further and information will be available that may help to answer some of them.

Differentiation

Less able
● Provide children with key words related to the picture, to help with spellings.
More able
● Encourage children to formulate questions that begin with other words besides those beginning with *wh*.

Teachers and lessons in Victorian times

Objectives

NLS

T1: To reinforce and apply their word-level skills through shared and guided reading.

T16: To scan a text to find specific sections, eg key words or phrases, subheadings.

W9: To learn new words from reading linked to particular topics.

What you need

● Photocopiable page 188.

Shared text-level work

● Remind the children about the pictures they looked at and the questions they raised. Explain that they will look at a text that may answer their questions.

● Show the text and ask the children to look for the subheadings *Teachers* and *Lessons*. Discuss the ideas they already have about these from research done so far.

● Read these paragraphs. Ask if any of the questions have been answered by reading the text.

● If any children still have unanswered questions, discuss how they might be able to find answers. For example, they could use books, the internet, posters and encyclopedias.

● Practise note-making skills by taking a complete sentence from the text and reducing it to note form. For example, *At the beginning of the day, the teacher would teach the lessons to some of the older children who then taught the younger ones during the day* could be reduced to *Teacher taught older children, older children then taught younger children.*

Shared word-level work

● Look with the children at *Reading, wRiting and aRithmetic*. Ask them if they can see why the Victorians referred to these subjects as the three Rs. Remind the children about differences between how we write and say some words. Talk about the *wr* beginning for words and ask the children if they know any other words that begin with *wr* (*wrong, wring, wren, wrap, wrist*, and so on), and write some examples on the board.

● Pick out difficult or unfamiliar words, such as *younger, earning, attacked, arithmetic, copying, especially, expected, slates* and *punished* and write these on the board, noting their spellings.

Guided and independent work

● Guide one group by discussing the text. Talk about key words and phrases and important information. Support the children's reading of this text and others to help them to scan for information about teachers and lessons.

● Ask the children to read about teachers and lessons in pairs and then make brief notes about it. Remind them that they need to be brief and that they should concentrate on noting key words rather than including articles (*the, a, an*) or writing sentences.

Differentiation

Less able

● Pair children who find the text difficult to read with more able readers, so that they can still understand the text.

More able

● Provide additional texts and access to websites so that children can extend their search.

Plenary

● Ask children to share the notes they made. Write some examples on the board and build up an abbreviated version of the text. Ask if any key points are missing and insert these in appropriate places.

● Look at the new text with the children and discuss it, using the notes as a starting point for giving information orally in sentences.

Slates, discipline and work

Objectives

NLS
T19: To make simple notes from non-fiction texts.
S4: To use commas in lists.
S5: To write in clear sentences using capital letters and full stops accurately.

What you need
● Photocopiable page 188.

Shared text-level work
● Begin by talking about the notes the children made in previous lessons. Discuss what they have already found out about life in Victorian schools.
● Show the children the new text, but before reading it, ask them to skim the text and then cover it before giving key information to partners and then to the rest of the class.
● Encourage them to make notes on whiteboards or paper on what they can recall from the text. Tell them that they can uncover the text to check their notes and spellings when they need to.
● Record their comments in note form on the board before reading the text with them.
● Ask the children to look at the notes and to help you to add to these now that they have read the text more carefully.

Shared word- and sentence-level work
● Again, notice unfamiliar words, such as *scratched, sharpened, sponges, sleeves, naughty, properly, dunce, factories, chimney, injured* and *period.* Discuss the meanings and challenge the children to use them in sentences.
● Ask the children to look at the notes on the board one by one and to suggest ways in which these could be written as simple sentences in their own words.
● Pay particular attention to the use of capital letters and full stops, and use commas wherever the sentences include lists.

Guided and independent work
● Guide a more able group as they write sentences based on the text and notes. Encourage them to look for ways to combine sentences so that they become more complex and interesting. Talk about words that can be used to link sentences (*and, but* and so on) and talk about using commas to list items so that more than one piece of information may be included in the same sentence. Explain that while complex sentences can make our writing more interesting, we should not make sentences too long as this can make reading complicated.
● Provide each pair of children with photocopiable page 188 and ask them to write simple sentences based on the notes made on the board and their own ideas.

Differentiation

Less able
● Give pairs of children some incomplete sentences to complete before they move on to working more independently. The first sentences could require children to insert only one word in order to complete them, but gradually more words and phrases might be omitted according to the ability of the children to complete them.

More able
● See Guided and independent work.

Plenary
● Ask the guided group to share some of their sentences with the class. Write a few of these on the board and talk about the features of the sentences. Talk, in particular, about the use of commas in lists.
● Revisit some of the new words to ensure that children thoroughly understand them.
● Ask them to help you to write sentences which include the new words, encouraging them to suggest where commas, full stops and capital letters should be placed.

Facts about Victorian schools

Objectives

NLS
T13: To understand the distinction between fact and fiction; to use terms 'fact', 'fiction' and 'non-fiction' appropriately.
S5: To write in clear sentences using capital letters and full stops accurately.
W10: To use synonyms and other alternative words/phrases that express same or similar meanings; to collect, discuss similarities and shades of meaning and use to extend and enhance writing.

What you need
● Photocopiable page 189
● resources on the Victorians.

Differentiation

Less able
● See Guided and independent work

More able
● Provide children with additional information sources, and ask them to write sentences with details of interesting facts they discover about Victorian schools.

Shared text-level work
● Look at the title of the text and ask the children if they can explain what is meant by *facts*. Write *fact, fiction* and *non-fiction* on the board and ask the children if they can explain them. Can they name an example text of each type?
● Make some statements and ask whether they represent facts, opinions or fiction. Which would appear in a fiction book and which in a non-fiction book? For example:

> ● London is the biggest city in England.
> ● Red is a nicer colour than green.
> ● Tuesday is the day after Monday.
> ● Merlin the magical puppy was wearing a magical collar.

● Ask the children to justify their choices and to make up further statements which could be facts, opinions or fiction.
● Explain that all of the statements in the text are facts. They will already have seen some of the information in previous texts, but here it is presented more concisely.
● Read the first statement. Ask if this could be fact, fiction or an opinion. (It's a fact.) Then make another statement: *It was a very good idea to make all children under 12 go to school in Victorian times.* Is this statement fact, opinion or fiction? Which words make it clear that this is opinion? Look at the rest of the sentences in the same way.

Shared word- and sentence-level work
● Talk about different words that could be used to replace some of those in the second sentence. How could the sentence be rewritten to sound better or simpler? For example, *named* instead of *called*, *orphans* instead of *children without parents*, *poor* instead of *with little money*.
● Look briefly at some of the other sentences and ask the children to suggest synonyms for some of the words and phrases.

Guided and independent work
● Work with the least able group to guide their rewriting of sentences and to discuss possible synonyms and alternative phrases. Choose the sentences for them.
● Ask the children to write different versions of the sentences, using synonyms. Divide the sentences between groups so that each child attempts a few.
● Those who complete these in time can go on to rewrite sentences allotted to other groups.

Plenary
● Share some of the sentences. Compare which aspects have been changed and what synonyms are used.
● Ask if the sentences represent fact, fiction or opinion. What clues can we use to work this out?

Writing under headings

Objectives

NLS

T17: To skim-read title, contents page, illustrations, chapter headings and subheadings, to speculate what a book might be about.

T20: To write non-fiction texts, using texts read as models for own writing, eg use of headings, subheadings.

S5: To write in clear sentences using capital letters and full stops accurately.

What you need

● Photocopiable pages 188 and 189

● additional information on Victorian schools

● the children's work so far.

Shared text-level work

● This lesson gives the opportunity for more extended writing about Victorian school life. You may wish to provide additional time.

● Write headings on the board relating to work done so far, such as *teachers, lessons, buildings, discipline.*

● Ask the children to tell you interesting things they have learned about Victorian education. As they do so, write the information in note form under the relevant heading. Encourage children to tell you the appropriate heading each time. If information doesn't belong under any of the headings, ask them to suggest additional headings such as *games* and *religion.*

● Discuss the functions of titles, headings and subheadings and explain that it is much easier to find information from text if these features are used. Talk about the different ways in which we read. For narrative, we read from beginning to end because otherwise we would miss important parts of a story. In non-fiction, we often want to find out about only one thing so we may begin reading in the middle of a text.

● Scan the photocopiable pages and discuss what they are about by referring to headings and subheadings.

Shared sentence-level work

● Talk about using notes to write a report, with subheadings to separate sections.

● Quickly check that the children remember that a sentence should have a capital letter and a full stop.

● Model reading the notes under one of the headings and selecting some to develop into sentences. Involve the children in composing and punctuating the sentences.

Guided and independent work

● Explore a variety of information sources on Victorian education. Discuss the ways in which they are set out and the information they provide. Do they cover similar topics? Do they make similar use of subheadings and illustrations?

● Ask the children to collate and read their work so far and to produce their own piece of writing about Victorian education. Remind them to use subheadings and write about a subject at a time in complete sentences.

● Explain that they may wish to find further information from books and the internet.

Differentiation

Less able

● Encourage children to contribute to the content, but give help with grammar and punctuation where necessary.

More able

● Encourage children to write in paragraphs.

Plenary

● Ask the children to show their work to partners who were not sitting with them during independent work. Invite children to talk about their colleagues' work.

● Write a few sentences on the board and check that they are written correctly. Ask the children what heading would be most suitable for each sentence to be written under.

UNIT 5 HOUR 7 ◻ Non-fiction 2: Report

Questions about playing outside

Objectives
NLS
T14: To pose questions and record these in writing, prior to reading non-fiction to find answers.
S6: To turn statements into questions, learning a range of 'wh' words typically used to open questions and to add question marks.
S&L
23 Group discussion and interaction: To work effectively in groups by ensuring each group member takes a turn, challenging, supporting and moving on

What you need
- Photocopiable page 190
- further resources on Victorian games, including internet access if possible.

Differentiation
More able
- Provide a challenging range of texts. If possible, ask some to word process their questions. Later, they could find answers on the internet and copy and paste these into their work.

Less able
- Ensure that children who are sometimes reticent are placed in sympathetic groups where they will have the opportunity to contribute.

Shared text-level work
- Explain that in the next four lessons the children will be looking at some of the toys and games that Victorian children enjoyed.
- Say that the text they will read next may answer some of the questions they may have, but that they will be able to find out more by looking at books and websites.
- Let the children discuss in pairs what they might like to know about the games Victorian children played outdoors. Write these on the board as full questions, for example *Did Victorian children ride bikes? Did Victorian children have football teams? Did Victorian children play skipping?*

Shared sentence-level work
- Now write the headings *Playground games, Playing in the street, Football,* and *Marbles.* Explain that these were some of the games that children played outside, and tell them that they will be reading about these things in the next lesson.
- Again, after a short thinking and chatting time, ask the children to suggest questions they would like answered about each subject in turn. Model writing their questions on the board, asking the children to suggest phrasing and punctuation. Encourage them to use the subheadings as a staring point for their questions: *What playground games did Victorian children play? Do we still play some of the same games now? Do we play them differently? Was it dangerous to play in the street? Why is it more dangerous to play in the street now than it was in Victorian times?*

Guided and independent work
- Work with a higher ability group to guide their question-writing based on the headings from shared work.
- Provide the children with additional texts and internet access, so that they can write additional questions for others to answer using the sources. Other children can then use the sources to find out answers.
- Provide small groups of children with a sheet of paper with the headings. Ask them to work together to discuss and write questions about each topic. Encourage them to discuss their questions with other group members and remind them of the importance of taking turns, listening to others, and keeping to the subject.

Plenary
- Ask the guided group to introduce the texts they looked at. If you have an electronic whiteboard, show some of the web pages.
- Look at the questions posed by the children, write some on the board, and see if the guided group can answer any of them.
- Remind children how to use contents, headings and subheadings (on the web as well as in print) to locate information.

Playing outside in Victorian times

Objectives
NLS
T19: To make simple notes from non-fiction texts, eg key words and phrases to use in subsequent writing.
W9: To learn new words from reading linked to particular topics, to build individual collections of personal interest or significant words.

What you need
● Photocopiable page 190.

Shared text-level work
● Encourage the children to skim-read the text and tell you what it is about. Do they notice that they might find answers to questions from the last lesson?
● Read the text and ask if anyone has found an answer to a question.
● Now look at the first sentence. Talk about what the word *variety* means, and explain that this text only describes a small number of the games Victorian children played. Also, it provides only brief information about the games and little description of how they were played.
● Ask the children how they think they could find out more, and remind them about the texts they looked at in the previous lesson.
● Look at the text again and highlight the following in the opening paragraph: *variety, hoops, hopscotch, hide and seek, jacks or fivestones.*
● Explain that you have picked out the key words in the text. Ask the children to look at the next paragraph and suggest which words could be highlighted as key points. They might pick out: *street, playground, no cars, horses and carriages were uncommon.* Explain that this is a way of making notes to help us to find important information.
● Stress that notes are only useful if we still understand what they mean when we look at them later, so sometimes we need to highlight more than one word. For example, if we only highlighted or wrote *cars,* we might forget that there were actually no cars or very few cars. Similarly, it is important to note that *horses and carriages* were *uncommon* in some places.
● Write the key words on the board for the first two sections.
● Finally, look at the sections in the text on *football* and *marbles* and ask the children to help you to pick out the key words. Write the key words on the board.

Shared word-level work
● Look at some of the less familiar words from the text and discuss these with the children, for example: *hopscotch, fivestones, pavement, playground, dangerous, carriages, uncommon, leather, bladder, wealthy, marble, alleys, knuckles, knucklebones* and *index.*
● When you have established their meanings, display the words prominently for reference.

Guided and independent work
● Divide the class into five groups. Ask the children to look at the notes left on the board and use them to write sentences about one of the topics. Encourage them to discuss what each group member will write.

Plenary
● Ask children from each group to read their report to the class.
● Encourage suggestions for additional information, and discuss layout features and general presentation.

Differentiation

Less able
● Discuss each sentence the children wish to write and, if necessary, scribe for them, asking them to dictate to you.

More able
● Provide additional texts if children wish to add extra information. Emphasise that they should scan for key words and phrases and should write in their own words.

Sunday games

Objectives
NLS
T19: To make simple notes from non-fiction texts, eg key words and phrases to use in subsequent writing.
W9: To learn new words from reading linked to particular topics.

What you need
● Photocopiable page 191
● additional resources on Victorian games.

Shared text-level work
● Recall knowledge about Victorian outdoor games, and explain to the children that in the next two lessons they will be finding out about Victorian *indoor* games.
● Explain that in the 19th century, most people in Britain were Christian and many more went to church than today. Sunday was regarded as a special day when people did not go work, the shops were closed and children were expected to be quiet and serious.
● Read the section on Sunday games. If the children do not know the story of Noah's Ark, talk to them about it.
● Ask the children to look at the text as you read it again, and to make notes of the key points.
● Now ask the children to share their notes. Some may have written very little, so ask pairs to first share their notes with another pair and allow them time to add to their notes.

Shared word-level work
● Focus on the religious terms in the text, for example *Bible, duty, Noah, verses, scripture, Celestial, Heaven.* Encourage children to offer explanations of their meanings, and then practise spellings.

Guided and independent work
● Re-read the paragraph with the children. Talk with them about the spellings of difficult or less familiar words in the text and help them to learn these by using *Look>Say>Cover>Write>Check*. Ask them to write them on cards, or ideally whiteboards, for use in the plenary.
● Encourage them to use the words in new sentences.
● Ask pairs of children to re-read the section about Sunday games and highlight the key words.
● Provide the children with a list of questions or, for the less able, sentences to complete. For example:

● Why was Sunday boring for many Victorian children?
● What games could children play on Sundays?
● What was a Noah's Ark?

● When the children have answered the questions, ask them to make up at least one question about the text for a colleague to answer.

Differentiation

Less able
● Provide cloze sentences about Sunday games and give children the word cards to help them.

More able
● Provide additional resources about the topic for children to make notes from.

Plenary
● Go over the answers to the questions.
● Let children ask any questions they made up themselves to the class. Model sentence-writing with the answers.
● Show the children the word cards/whiteboards and ask them to say the word as you hold up each one.
● Then hand out the cards and ask the children to hold the cards in front of them when you mention their word. Ask questions such as, *Who has the word 'scripture'? Who is holding the word 'Bible'?*

Dolls and mechanical toys

Objectives
NLS
T20: To write non-fiction texts, using texts read as models for own writing, eg use of headings, sub-headings, captions.
S5: To write in clear sentences using capital letters and full stops accurately.

What you need
● Photocopiable page 191
● additional resources on Victorian toys and dolls.

Shared text-level work
● For this final lesson, there are two items on indoor toys to read about. Some children may already have looked at these in the previous lesson and have some ideas about the content.
● Write the headings *Dolls* and *Mechanical toys* on the board and talk about each. Emphasise that dolls are not necessarily girls' toys. Remind them about dolls/figures such as Action Man. Similarly, some may feel that mechanical toys are for boys only. While this tended to be the case in Victorian times, many girls today enjoy playing with such toys.
● Read the text with the children and discuss the content. Ask questions about each section, for example:

> What kind of materials were Victorian dolls made from?
> How was the motor wound up on a clockwork railway engine?
> Why did Victorian children need to be very careful when they played with wax or china dolls?
> Can you name some different clockwork toys?

● Write some of their answers under the two headings.

Guided and independent work
● Allocate half the class to work about dolls and half mechanical toys (make sure the split isn't by gender).
● Ask the children to work together in pairs or small groups to identify and discuss key words in the text and to make notes about their topic.
● Explain that at the end of the lesson people who have been studying each of the topics will report back to the class on what they have found out so that everyone will know more about both topics.
● Emphasise that, at this stage, the children need only make notes and that the whole class will help turn some of the notes into sentences in the plenary session.

Plenary
● Let the groups report on what they have found out. Encourage children to listen to each other carefully and to comment on each other's reports.
● Ask the class to suggest some key pieces of information that should be included in a piece of writing about dolls or mechanical toys.
● Develop these into sentences on the board with the children's help. Note correct punctuation and discuss sentence structure and ways of improving the sentences where appropriate. Remind the children to use words such as *and* and *but* to link sentences but not to make their sentences too long. Ensure that the children are being imaginative with their vocabulary and thinking of interesting synonyms.
● Ask children to write up their reports on Victorian toys. Provide additional resources for them to consult. Ask them to conclude their reports with a brief comparison of Victorian and modern toys and to say which are better and which Victorian toys they might like to play with.

Differentiation
Less able
● Ensure that children are fully involved in the group discussions and encourage them to present if they feel confident.

More able
● Provide additional resources so children become 'experts' on dolls or mechanical toys and can share their knowledge with other groups.

TERM 3

Victorian school life

A Victorian schoolroom

Going to school in Victorian times

Some schools which children go to today were built over a hundred years ago. From the outside, they often look much as they did in Victorian times. Inside, schools were quite different and not nearly as pleasant as they are now.

Teachers

Often, one teacher taught almost all the children in the school in one large room. At the beginning of the day, the teacher would teach the lessons to older children who then taught the younger ones during the day. Some parents did not want their children to go to school and thought they should work to earn money instead.

Lessons

Most lessons were about the three Rs (Reading, wRiting and aRithmetic). Often children copied pages from the Bible. They were expected to write neatly on slates or paper and were punished if they made mistakes. Instead of PE, children did drill, in which they marched up and down. Lessons lasted from 9am to 5pm, with a two-hour lunch break.

Slates

Children wrote on slates. They were a bit like the mini whiteboards which many children use today. Some children brought sponges in, but many spat on the slates and cleaned them with their sleeves.

Discipline

When children were naughty, teachers hit them with canes. Children who could not do their work properly were often made to stand in the corner wearing a dunce's cap.

Going to school

For many years, most children did not go to school at all. Children as young as five had to work. Many worked in factories, on farms or as chimney sweeps. Many children were injured or even killed at work. By the end of the Victorian period, all children between 5 and 12 had to go to school.

Victorian schools

● By the end of the Victorian age, all children under 12 had to go to school.

● Some schools were called 'ragged' schools. These were for orphans and very poor children.

● Curtains were used to divide the school into classrooms.

● Often school managers did not spend much money on repairs, so buildings were left to rot.

● Lessons in Victorian schools mainly concentrated on the 'three Rs' – Reading, wRiting and aRithmetic.

● Lessons lasted from 9am to 5pm, with a two-hour lunch break.

● Children learned to write on slates. They scratched letters on them with sharpened pieces of slate. Slates could be used again and again so this saved money.

● Children had to bring sponges from home to clean their slates, but many just spat on the slates and then wiped them with their sleeves.

● When children were naughty, many teachers hit them with sticks called canes. Girls were caned on their hands, but boys were caned on their bottoms.

● Children who could not do their work properly were often made to stand in the corner of the classroom wearing a dunce's cap.

● For PE, children learned to march to music. This was called 'drill'.

Victorian outdoor games

Playground games

Victorian children played a variety of outdoor games. Some played with large hoops which they bowled along the ground. The hoops were like the hula hoops which we still use today, and children used a short stick to tap them with to keep them rolling. Children also played hopscotch, hide and seek, and jacks or 'fivestones'. For fivestones, they used a small bouncy ball and either five small pebbles, or five pig's knucklebones.

Football

Most children were too poor to be able to afford to buy a football, which would be made of leather, so they would ask the butcher for a pig's bladder which they would blow up and use as a ball.

Street games

For many children, the pavement of their street would be their usual playground and meeting place. Of course there were no cars to make this a dangerous place to play, and in many streets even horses and carriages were an uncommon sight.

Marbles

Victorian children from wealthy families played with marbles made from real marble. Poorer children played with marbles made from glass. Marbles were sometimes called alleys. To 'shoot' a marble they put their knuckles on the ground and placed the marble on their index finger. Then they flicked their thumbs and made the marble shoot along the ground.

Victorian indoor games

Sunday games

For many Victorian children, Sunday could be a very long and boring day. They were not allowed to read books or play with any of their weekday toys. On a Sunday they could only read Bible stories or play games that reminded them of their duty to make this a day of rest. For this reason, toy Noah's Arks were very popular, because children could enjoy playing with all the animals while still thinking about the Bible. For older children, there were card games that involved learning verses of scripture, or board games in which the players would race to reach the Promised Land or the Celestial City (Heaven)!

Dolls

The most common dolls were those made of cloth, which were usually called rag dolls. Many children also played with little wooden dolls called Dutch dolls, which had jointed arms and legs. Little girls from rich families would have had some dolls whose heads, arms and legs were made from wax or from china. These dolls would have had glass eyes and real hair on their heads, and frilly clothes trimmed with lace. Of course, they were very expensive and fragile and so they were usually treated with great care. A wax doll could melt if she was left too near the fire, and a china doll would break if dropped!

Mechanical toys

There were no battery-powered or electronic games for children, but a lucky child might have had a clockwork toy train. When the motor had been wound up using a big key which fitted in the side of the engine, the train would run round and round the tracks. The real railways were still very modern and exciting, so a toy railway was a wonderful thing to play with. There were many other kinds of clockwork toys, usually made from tin. When the key was wound, a clockwork soldier might march, or a musician bang his drum, or a pair of boxers might punch each other!